Building Academic Reading Skills

BOOK 2

Dorothy Zemach

Ann Arbor
The University of Michigan Press

Acknowledgments

Grateful acknowledgment is made to the following authors, publishers, and individuals for permission to reprint previously published materials beyond fair use guidelines.

Malcolm Gladwell for permission to use material from *Outliers: The Story of Success,* published by Little, Brown. Copyright 2008.

Julia Harvey of South Eugene High School, Eugene, OR, for her help with the contents of Unit 3.

Kenneth G. Libbrecht, Professor of Physics and Physics Executive Officer, California Institute of Technology, www.its.caltech.edu/–atomic/snowcrystals/, for information and diagrams used in Unit 2.

Dr. Pamela Ronald, University of California–Davis (http://indica.ucdavis.edu), for her help and advice on the material in Unit 6.

Every effort has been made to contact the copyright holders for permission to reprint borrowed material. We regret any oversights that may have occurred and will rectify them in future printings of this book.

ISBN-13: 978-0-472-03383-6

2013   2012   2011   2010   4   3   2   1

Contents

To the Instructor

Native speakers of English and those learning English as a second or foreign language are often surprised to learn that there are reading "skills"; that is, that reading is more than literacy and a large vocabulary. However, practicing and using a variety of reading skills will help a student read faster, have better comprehension, and retain and apply the information more effectively. Although there are many skills-based texts available, *Building Academic Reading Skills* offers pre-reading, during reading, and post-reading development activities in all units and for each reading within a unit. For example, students will practice **skimming** and **scanning** for almost all twelve readings in the book.

Building Academic Reading Skills teaches academic reading skills, those most useful for college and university students. It assumes that students will be coping with significant amounts of reading, different types of texts, academic vocabulary, and difficult subject matter.

Each unit features one topic treated by two different academic disciplines (for a total of 12). For example, Unit 4 focuses on plastic, first with a passage from a medical textbook, and then with an editorial letter from a newspaper. The units contain both textbook readings and readings from other genres since students are increasingly reading newspaper, magazine, journal, and online articles in addition to their textbooks. The readings, while adapted to be accessible to high-intermediate students, are not easy. However, through the systematic application of the reading skills, students will be able to understand them and apply the information they learn. Students will gain the satisfaction of having engaged with and mastered challenging texts.

In each unit, students will

- discuss general questions about the topic to prepare for both readings.
- learn and practice vocabulary and reading skills relevant to the first reading. Some skills—such as predicting, skimming, and scanning—are practiced in every unit.
- read the reading first without using a dictionary. In some units they will identify words to look up later. This helps students discriminate between necessary and unnecessary vocabulary in reading, which builds fluency.
- answer questions about the reading's main ideas. This helps students recognize that they can understand the important ideas of a reading even if they don't know the meaning of every word in the passage.
- answer questions about the reading's details. This helps students improve their reading comprehension.

- look up or infer through guided exercises the meaning of additional vocabulary.
- read the reading a second time.
- apply the reading skill taught in the lesson.
- apply the information to broader areas through exercises or group discussions.
- repeat the process with the second reading in the unit and extend their learning with final discussion questions that allow students, where appropriate, to integrate the information from the two different fields of study.

Students learn vocabulary relevant to each reading and the broader topic, but more importantly, they learn strategies for coping with the amount of vocabulary they can expect to encounter in academic texts. Often, they practice choosing a limited number of words to check in a dictionary and then, after they have looked up the words, analyze whether they made good choices. (The number of words students look up varies depending on other vocabulary skills taught in the lesson.) Additionally, students answer questions about the main idea of the passage before working with specific vocabulary; in this way, students become more confident about their ability to understand a passage even when they don't know the meaning of every word.

The readings are progressively more difficult, and skills learned in earlier units are recycled in subsequent units as possible. Therefore, while it is not required to do every unit or to do them in order, it is strongly encouraged because students like to see that they are making progress and that they are able to handle increasingly difficult readings over time.

Robots

Discuss

Discuss these questions with a small group.

1. What is a robot? Write a definition and give some examples.

2. What are some things that robots are used for now? What do you think might be done by robots in the future?

3. Have you seen any movies or read any books that had robots as characters? Describe one or two of them. What did they look like? How did they act? Do you think robot characters are usually good, usually evil, or that there is no pattern?

4. What are some things that robots can do better than people? What are some things that people can do better than robots?

Reading 1: Film Studies

Pre-Reading Activities

Reading Skills Overview

Complete the passage about reading skills using terms from the box. Do not change the word forms.

context	inferences	signposts
definitions	opinions	skim
conclusions	pronouns	scan
examples	scan	transitions

Academic reading is different from reading for pleasure. While sometimes vocabulary can be more difficult, the good news is that there are many features of academic texts that help the reader. For example, many textbooks use ① _____ such as headings to name sections and **bold** and *italics* to signal important terms. Important new words are often explained by ② _____ that are given directly, often set off by punctuation such as commas, dashes, or parentheses. The writer might also give ③ _____ to make the meaning even clearer.

Because academic reading is usually non-fiction and does not have a story or a plot, you don't need to start at the beginning and read through to the end. In fact, good readers often look at the text twice. The first time, they ④ _____ it very quickly to get a general idea of what it is about, how long it is, how difficult it is, and some of the main points. They read the title, headings, and the first and last sentences of each paragraph. Then they go back and read the text carefully. Even though it sounds like this procedure takes more time than just reading through once, you might be surprised to find that it actually saves time because readers will understand the text better and remember the information more easily.

Sometimes you don't need to read everything carefully. You might be looking for just one or two pieces of specific information such as a date or a name. In that case, you can just ⑤ _____ the text for that information without reading the whole text.

If you do need to read carefully, pay attention to ⑥ _____ such as *first, next, finally, therefore, because, before, while, after,* and *these days* that show relationships and connections between ideas. Understanding these relationships will make it easier for you to understand the writer's ideas. If you see ⑦ _____ such as *it, they, she, those,* and so on, make sure that you know which people, places, and ideas they refer to.

Sometimes you can figure out the meaning of vocabulary from ⑧ _____; other times, you will need to use your dictionary. However, it's important to remember that you probably won't have time to look up every new word that you encounter. Instead, learn to recognize which words are necessary for understanding the overall meaning of the text.

It can be difficult when reading to identify when the writer is using facts and when he or she is expressing ⑨ _____. However, you will probably read many academic articles that have a strong point of view. Sometimes these are stated directly, and sometimes they are more indirect, leaving you as the reader to make ⑩ _____. Whether you are reading mostly facts, mostly opinions, or a mixture of both, your instructor will expect you to draw ⑪ _____ about the subject when you finish reading.

Vocabulary

Match the common word pair, or collocation, on the left to its definition, or meaning, on the right.

1. science fiction

2. classic example

3. comic relief

4. good guys

5. human beings

6. nuclear weapon

7. plot twist

8. bad guys

9. technological advances

10. widely accepted

a. a character or scene in a serious movie that makes audiences laugh as a way to relieve dramatic tension

b. a famous or common model or typical representation of something

c. people

d. an unexpected change in a story's direction

e. believed by most people to be true

f. literary fantasy that explores the impact of technology on society

g. modern inventions from science and industry

h. the bad characters in a book or movie

i. the good characters in a book or movie

j. something that uses nuclear energy to explode

Predict

Work with a partner. Look at the title and subtitles of the reading (pages 6–8). This reading describes images of robots in different films. How do you think the text will be organized? Discuss your ideas, and then circle your guess.

    a. by popularity (from most popular movies to least popular movies)

    b. by date (chronologically; from oldest movies to most recent movies)

    c. by category (first movies with good robots; then movies with evil robots)

    d. by nationality (first movies from one country; then movies from another country)

    e. by quality (from worst quality to best quality)

Skim

Skim the reading quickly. Check the headings. Read the topic sentence of each paragraph. Then circle your answers to the questions.

    1. The reading will be *easy / medium / difficult* for me to understand.

    2. The reading contains *mostly facts / mostly opinions / a mix of facts and opinions*.

    3. Check your answer to the Predict question. Was your answer correct?

Scan

Find the answers to these questions as quickly as you can. Raise your hand to show your instructor when you have finished.

    1. When was the word *robot* first used? _____

    2. How many main images of robots does the article describe? _____

    3. What is the name of the robot in the movie *Forbidden Planet*? _____

    4. How many "Laws of Robotics" are there? _____

    5. Who directed the movie *2001: A Space Odyssey*? _____

    6. What is the name of the movie that was made in 1982? _____

Read

Read the excerpt from a textbook. Do NOT check the meanings of any words in a dictionary yet; some of them will be used for activities following the reading. You will be able to look them up in a dictionary later.

Images of Robots in Film

1 It's difficult to pinpoint the first mention of robots in literature; even the *Iliad* and the *Odyssey* of ancient Greece contained descriptions of large machine-like creatures. The word *robot* itself, though, dates to 1921, when it was used in Czech author Karel Capek's play *R.U.R.* (*Rossum's Universal Robots*). The word itself derives from the Czech word for work or labor, *robota*. The play told the story of mechanical workers who helped the men who built them until a scientist found a way to give them emotions, at which point they turned against the humans and tried to take over the world.

2 The first appearance of a robot in a movie was in 1926, in *Metropolis*, which featured Maria, a robotic copy (evil) of a real woman (good).

3 Robots grew in popularity in films as technological advances in society made their eventual existence seem more believable, as advances in automation made workers worry about the future of their jobs, and after the invention of nuclear weapons and other machines of war provoked fear of destruction.

4 Robots in film don't all look the same, of course, or act the same, but there are general categories into which most of them fall.

The Good Helper

5 Robots can be basically good; that is, helpers of humans. They might use their superior force or logical, computer-based reasoning to perform more capably than humans. This version appeals to people who see mankind's creations as useful and the advances of technology as good.

6 One of the earliest and also the most famous of the good helper robots is Robby the Robot from the 1956 film *Forbidden Planet*. Robby's classic design influenced generations of future movie and television

Figure 1.1 Robby the Robot from "Forbidden Planet"

robots, and in fact Robby himself was reused in other films and shows. The name Robby probably comes from a short story written by science fiction author Isaac Asimov in 1940 that featured a robot named Robbie. A collection of stories by Asimov in 1950 called *I, Robot* introduced the idea of the Three Laws of Robotics:

1. A robot may not injure a human being or, through inaction, allow a human being to come to harm.

2. A robot must obey any orders given to it by human beings, except where such orders would conflict with the First Law.

3. A robot must protect its own existence as long as such protection does not conflict with the First or Second Law.

Figure 1.2 C-3PO from "Star Wars"

These three laws came to be widely accepted by writers and filmmakers alike for generations, although surprisingly no film version of Asimov's landmark stories was made until the 2004 movie *I, Robot*.

7 A variation on this good type of robot involves a plot twist where the robot, either through a mechanical failure or through interference from a human bad guy, temporarily becomes evil and must be restored to its original helpful state.

8 The good helper robot is also used as comic relief, with its inability to understand emotional humans, humans' metaphorical language, and human relationships. C-3PO of the *Star Wars* movies, who first appeared in 1977, falls into this category, and is used throughout the series to add a lighter element to the ongoing struggle between good and evil.

The Evil Threat

9 A more dramatic type of robot is the one bent on the destruction of mankind. There are several variations to this type of robot too. The most basic one is a robot used by the bad guys to fight the good guys; think of the army of Sentinels in *The Matrix* (1999) or the Terminator played so effectively by Arnold Schwarzenegger in *Terminator 1* (1984).

10 An interesting recurring theme is that of the robot that "learns to think" and then turns on its creators. HAL, the murderous spaceship computer in Stanley Kubrick's 1968 masterpiece *2001: A Space Odyssey,* fits this pattern neatly. Sometimes the robot is destroyed by humans, and in a not-so-uncommon twist, sometimes the robot is convinced to destroy itself by being made to realize that it is dangerous.

11 Not surprisingly, this type of robot is popular with people who feel apprehensive about technology's place in society; perhaps they don't understand it or are worried about potential problems from the misuse of machines.

The Pseudo-Human

12 In this category we have both the *android*, a type of robot that has such human features that it looks just a like a person, and the *cyborg*, a part human/part robot mix. These robots that look human can be basically good, such as Commander Data of the television show (1987-1994) and movie series (late '90s–early 2000s) *Star Trek: The Next Generation*; but often they are evil, and much of the plot of the movie revolves around the other characters or even the film-watching audience not knowing which characters are human and which are machines. A classic example of this type of robot is found in the 1975 movie *The Stepford Wives* (which was remade in 2004) that featured a town of "perfect" wives who turned out to be robots. The 1982 film *Blade Runner* featured androids known as "replicants," one of whom did not know that she wasn't human.

Fig. 1.3 The 1975 Stepford Wives

13 This type of robot appeals to those who see something positive in adding technology to the human body; to them, it's an extension of advances in medicine such as artificial limbs. On the other hand, those who fear that society is becoming too dependent on automation and technology love to be scared by the idea of robots slowly replacing humans.

Post-Reading Activities

Main Ideas

Circle the answer that best expresses the main ideas of the reading.

1. What is the main idea of the reading?
   a. Different types of robots in movies reflect different attitudes in movie makers and audience members.
   b. The image of robots in movies has changed over the years.
   c. There are only three different kinds of robots in movies.

2. Why are the Three Laws of Robotics important?
   a. They specify rules that every robot that appears in a movie must follow.
   b. They explain how society views robots in general.
   c. They influence the way that many robots behave in books and movies.

Details

Write the dates of the movies and books on the lines after the titles. Then number them in chronological order on the lines before the titles. One has been done for you as an example.

___ *2001: A Space Odyssey* _____

___ *Blade Runner* _____

___ *Forbidden Planet* _____

___ *I, Robot* (the book) _____

___ *I, Robot* (the movie) _____

___ *Metropolis* _____

_1_ *R.U.R. (Rossum's Universal Robots)* __1921__

___ *Star Trek: The Next Generation* (first television season) _____

___ *Star Wars* _____

___ *The Matrix* _____

___ *The Stepford Wives* (original) _____

___ *The Stepford Wives* (remake) _____

___ *The Terminator* _____

Reading Skills: Overview

Use different reading skills to answer the questions.

1. In Paragraph 1, what are the *Iliad* and the *Odyssey* examples of?

   a. Greek cities

   b. names of robots

   c. works of literature

2. Read Paragraph 1 again. What does the word *robota* mean?

   a. robot

   b. work or labor

   c. workers

3. In this sentence, the underlined word refers to _____ .

   The play told the story of mechanical workers who helped the men who built them until a scientist found a way to give them emotions, at which point <u>they</u> turned against the humans and tried to take over the world.

4. Read this sentence. What does the underlined word mean?

   These three laws came to be widely accepted by writers and filmmakers alike for generations, although surprisingly no film version of Asimov's <u>landmark</u> stories was made until the 2004 movie *I, Robot*.

   a. important

   b. very large or long

   c. old-fashioned

5. Read this sentence. What does the underlined expression mean?

> A more dramatic type of robot is the one <u>bent on</u> the destruction of mankind.

a. changed from its original purpose for

b. created for the purpose of

c. very focused on

6. True or false? Evil robots tend to have larger roles in movies than good robots.

_____

7. What are androids and cyborgs examples of?

a. robots that look like humans

b. evil robots

c. robots who do not realize that they are robots

8. In Paragraph 13, what two groups are contrasted by the phrase *On the other hand?*

a. good robots and bad robots

b. people who like technology and people who are afraid of technology

c. androids and robots that don't look like humans

Vocabulary

Read the article again. You may use a dictionary to look up any words. Write the words and their definitions. After you write each one, make a check (✓) after the definition if it was important to know the meaning of that word in order to understand the reading. Make an X after the definition if the word was not important.

Word	Definition	✓ or X

Understanding the Text

Discuss these questions with a partner or small group.

1. Why did the article mention books as well as movies?

2. Why did the writer group the robots by type instead of writing about the movies in chronological order?

3. How do you think the writer chose which movies to discuss?

Extension

Discuss these questions with a small group.

1. Read the television descriptions for these shows. What do you imagine the robots will be like?

The Day the Earth Stood Still (1951)

Watch the original classic! An alien lands on earth, bringing with him the powerful robot Gort. When a nervous U.S. Army soldier shoots and wounds the alien, Gort fights back. The alien is taken to a hospital, but later escapes and moves in with an Earth family. Eventually the alien reveals to the family that Gort's and his true purpose is to bring peace to the planet. But will they be able to succeed?

Artificial Intelligence: A.I. (2001)

Director Steven Spielberg's touching story of a robotic 11-year-old boy, David, who has been programmed to feel emotions. Bought by a family to replace their sick son, David is no longer wanted when their son is cured and comes home. To escape destruction, David runs away to try to find a way to become a real boy.

---

2. Have you seen any of the movies mentioned in the reading? What do you remember about the robots in them?

Reading 2: Sociology

Pre-Reading Activities

Understanding Transitions

Transitions link ideas. They show relationships between two or more elements in a sentence. They might link just two words, two groups of words, two sentences, or even two paragraphs. Sometimes a transition is followed by a comma.

> cyborgs **and** androids

> Scientist Joseph Engleberger said, "I can't define a robot, **but** I know one when I see one."

> Sometimes the robot is destroyed by humans, and in a not-so-uncommon twist, sometimes the robot is convinced to destroy itself by being made to realize that it is dangerous.
> **Not surprisingly**, this type of robot is popular with people who feel apprehensive about technology's place in society; perhaps they don't understand it or are worried about potential problems from the misuse of machines.

Understanding the use of transitions in a text helps you understand the writer's ideas. Transitions can show you what the writer considers important, the order in which events happened, or causes and effects.

Some common transition words and phrases and their meanings are listed.

> *Although / Though / But / However / In contrast / On the other hand / Rather / Then* highlight a contrast or an important difference. Typically, the most important idea is mentioned second.

> idea + transition + more important idea

> Most people think of robots as a modern invention. **However**, the first robot was actually created in 1206 by the Muslim inventor Al-Jazari.

Sometimes these transitions are used together, with one indicating how things were in the past and another signaling how things are today or will be in the future. If only the present or the future is highlighted with a transition, it is still likely that a past situation was discussed previously. Make sure you know which time period is the one that is most important for the main idea of the reading.

At first / Before / In years past / Traditionally are used to talk about the past.

In modern times / Recently / These days / Today / Now are used to talk about the present.

Down the road, / In (two years), / In the future, / Later, / Soon, are used to talk about the future.

In the future, *robots may be used more and more in homes across the country.*

As well as / For example, / For instance, / Furthermore, / In addition, / In other words, / Moreover, / Such as / That is (to say) offer examples or explanations and often follow definitions or complex ideas to make them easier to understand. Expressions that offer additional information usually signal the most important point. If writers are listing several features or ideas, they often put the most important idea last so that it will stand out.

Technological machines like computers may be actual robots in the future. **In addition***, cars or even home appliances,* **such as** *toasters, may become more advanced.*

Fortunately, / Unfortunately, / Luckily, / Strangely, / Surprisingly, show a writer's attitude toward an idea. Usually used at the beginning of a sentence, they can show a contrast between ideas.

idea + transition + new idea

Robots have the potential to perform many useful tasks that are too dangerous for humans. **Unfortunately***, the great expense of developing complex robots has limited their creation.*

Practice with Transitions

Read the passage. Circle the best transition.

Tired of doing housework? Dreaming of a time in the future when robots will do all your work for you? We might not have robots who can replace humans yet, but ① (**luckily / moreover**) there are some robots that you can buy to clean your home right now. The company iRobot sells several different models of household robots at affordable prices. ② (**Recently / For instance**), the little Roomba®, which looks something like a thick Frisbee®, will vacuum your floors for you. All you do is press a button, and it scoots across your floor, works around table and chair legs, and turns around if it hits a wall. With a special sensor you can mark off open doorways and staircases, so the Roomba stays in one area. You don't have to lift a finger. ③ (**Furthermore / Later**), you don't even have to watch it. You can simply set the controls and leave the room because the Roomba® will turn itself off when it's finished.

④ (**Soon / However**), my favorite model from iRobot is the Scooba®. This little robot actually washes floors using soap and water. ⑤ (**Surprisingly / In other words**), it did a better job than my husband! According to the manufacturer's website, the Scooba® removes up to 98 percent of bacteria. It even knows how to avoid carpets ⑥ (**as well as / such as**) stairs.

⑦ (**These days / In the future**), we may be able to purchase robots to do even more difficult chores. But for now, I'm happy with the helpers I have—and with my clean floors.

Predict

Talk with a partner. The reading (pages 18–19) is about a robot that is used with elderly patients in hospitals and nursing homes. Look at the title and photo on page 18. What do you think the robot does? What are its effects on patients?

Skim

Skim the reading quickly. Read the topic sentence of each paragraph. Then circle your answers to the questions.

1. The reading will be *easy / medium / difficult* for me to understand.

2. The reading contains *mostly facts / mostly opinions / a mix of facts and opinions*.

3. The reading has *a lot of / some / almost no* dates, figures, and statistics.

Scan

Find the answers to these questions as quickly as you can. Raise your hand to show your instructor when you have finished.

1. What is the robot's name? _____

2. When was it invented? _____

3. How many main effects is it designed to have? _____

4. How much does one cost? _____

Read

Read the article from a magazine. Underline any words that you want to look up in a dictionary.

A Different Kind of "Doctor"

1 Paro is a robot. Not the kind of robot who pilots a spaceship across the galaxy, nor the type who vacuums your floor, nor a child's toy. Paro, rather, is a type of robot known as a "mental commitment robot," a robot designed to interact with human beings on an emotional level. Created in 1993 by Takanori Shibata, a researcher at the Japanese company AIST (National Institute of Advanced Industrial Science and Technology), Paro has been used in hospitals, nursing homes, and even private homes in Japan, Europe, and the U.S.

2 Shaped like a baby harp seal, Paro looks at first like a stuffed animal. However, it has tactile, audition, light, temperature, and posture sensors that enable it to interact with humans. The tactile sensor lets Paro feel being touched by a person. If you pet Paro (similar to the way you would pet a dog or cat, for example), Paro will "remember" the action it did just before that and will repeat the action in the future to encourage you to pet it again. On the other hand, if you hit Paro, it will avoid its previous action to keep from being hit again. Touching Paro's whiskers will cause it to turn its head away, as if in shyness, or even cry. Paro can tell what direction a voice is coming from, recognize words such as its name, greetings,

A robot or a real seal?

and words of praise, and can respond by moving its head and legs, blinking its eyes, or making sounds. Using its light sensors, Paro becomes more active during the day and less active at night.

3 A robot such as Paro is designed to provide three main types of effects: (1) psychological, such as comforting people and encouraging them to take an interest in their lives and surroundings; (2) physiological, such as lowering blood pressure and alleviating the negative effects of stress; and (3) social, such as encouraging patients to talk with others, including their caregivers, and make friends.

4 Therapy with live animals has been used for years, and medical studies have documented the physical and psychological benefits. However, using animals in such settings can also be problematic. The animals themselves need special care, for example, and some patients might be allergic to them. Furthermore, as with any animal, no matter how gentle, there is a risk of biting or scratching if the animal becomes upset or scared, and some patients may be afraid of animals. An animal needs to be fed, too, as well as cleaned and exercised. Paro, in contrast, doesn't eat or need to be taken for a walk, and its artificial yet realistic fur is easy to clean. Paro will also stay with a patient for as long as the patient is interested; it can't get up and walk away.

5 Because of its relatively young age, only short-term studies have been carried out; encouragingly, these experiments have shown positive results on the mental health of some elderly people. In 2009, researchers at the Danish Techno-logical Institute's Centre for Robot Technology began a long-term study that should give more information about Paro's impact and usefulness. Those who have watched patients interact with Paro, though, are convinced that there are positive effects. They say the patients smile and talk more, and clearly look forward to Paro's visits.

6 As the Paros, which cost about $6000 each, become more widespread, more information will become available about their effects as well as their potential. Shibata is already working on new versions, although they won't be available for several years. There is hope that specialized versions of Paro could be created for certain groups of people, such as those suffering from autism or Alzheimer's.

Post-Reading Activities

Main Ideas

Check (✓) the statements that best express the main ideas of the readings.

_____ Paro was invented in Japan.

_____ Paro is used in hospitals and nursing homes.

_____ Paro can respond to sound, light, temperature, position, and touch.

_____ Paro doesn't like to have its whiskers touched.

_____ Paro provides psychological, physiological, and emotional effects.

_____ Not all patients like animals.

_____ No long-term studies on Paro's effectiveness have been carried out yet.

_____ Paro costs $6000.

Details

Read the statements. Write T if the statement is true and F if the statement is false.

1. Paros have only been used in hospitals and nursing homes. _____

2. Paros have been used in Asia, Europe, and North America. _____

3. Paro is available in several different animal shapes and colors. _____

4. Paro doesn't like being hit. _____

5. Paro can tell the difference between day and night. _____

6. Some patients who interact with Paro become more talkative. _____

7. Paro has some advantages over live animals. _____

8. The Danish Techological Institute recently finished a long-term study on Paro. _____

9. There will be updated versions of Paro in the future. _____

Vocabulary

Write answers to the questions. Then discuss them with a partner.

1. Did you underline any words to look up? If so, choose up to six that you think are important and look them up. Write the words and their definitions.

   a. _____

   b. _____

   c. _____

   d. _____

   e. _____

   f. _____

2. Were the words you chose to look up important in understanding the reading? Why or why not? Share your choices with a partner and explain why you think the words are important for understanding the reading or why you wish you had chosen other words.

Reading Skills: Understanding Transitions

Circle the best answer.

1. What does the word *rather* show in Paragraph 1?
   a. Paro is a different kind of robot from the examples in the previous sentence.
   b. Paro is one of many types of common robots.

2. What does the word *however* show in Paragraph 2?
   a. Paro is similar to a stuffed animal.
   b. Paro is different from a stuffed animal.

3. What does the expression *On the other hand* show in Paragraph 2?
   a. a difference between what Paro likes and what Paro doesn't like
   b. how Paro reacts to one of its five different sensors

4. What does the expression *such as* show in Paragraph 3?

   a. Paro is a very important type of robot.

   b. There are other robots similar to Paro.

5. What word in Paragraph 4 shows that animals have some significant disadvantages?

   _____

6. What expression in Paragraph 4 is used to explain the word *problematic*?

   _____

7. What expression in Paragraph 4 shows that Paro doesn't have these disadvantages?

   _____

8. What word in Paragraph 5 shows the writer's attitude toward the short-term studies on Paro?

   _____

Understanding the Text

Discuss these questions with a partner or small group.

1. Animals are often referred to as *he* or *she*. In this article, the writer refers to Paro as *it*. What may be the reason for that?

2. Why did the writer put quotation marks around the word *remember* in this sentence?

   > If you pet Paro (similar to the way you would pet a dog or cat, for example), Paro will "remember" the action it did just before that and will repeat the action in the future to encourage you to pet it again.

3. Does the writer believe that Paro is useful? How do you know?

4. According to Reading 1, what type of robot is Paro?

Extension

Discuss these questions with a partner or a small group, or write a paragraph response for each.

1. Assume that a patient is not allergic to or afraid of real animals. Do you think a real animal or a Paro would be more beneficial? Why?

2. Do you think people would like to keep robots such as Paro as pets? Why or why not?

3. Are there any disadvantages to using something such as Paro with patients? If so, what are they?

4. Do you think a robot such as Paro should be designed to look just like a human? Why or why not?

Snow

Discuss

Discuss these questions with a small group.

1. Describe some of your experiences with snow. Can you remember the first time you saw snow?

2. What are some positive aspects of snow? What are some negative aspects of snow or problems caused by snow?

3. What does a snowflake look like? Without looking ahead, draw an example of a snowflake and compare it with your other group members' drawings.

4. What is the value of studying poetry in high school and at a university? Why do some people enjoy poetry? Why do others not enjoy poetry? Discuss possible reasons. Do you personally enjoy poetry? Why or why not?

Reading 1: Physics

Pre-Reading Activities

Understanding and Using Charts and Illustrations

Many academic readings, particularly in math and the sciences, contain charts and illustrations. These "pictures" break up the written text, but they are not just decoration or a chance to rest your eyes. Charts, graphs, and diagrams or illustrations are important tools to help you understand the material. Sometimes they may give information that is not included in the text. Other times, they illustrate the information in a visual way that can greatly help your understanding.

If a diagram or chart is also explained in words in the text, then the words are still important. On a test, you may need to draw a diagram; you may need to label a diagram or illustration: or you may need to explain a process or idea in words. Therefore, it is important that you be able to understand the information both visually and through words.

As an example, read this explanation of a simple physics concept, the working of a lever.

A lever is a rigid object that when used with a **fulcrum,** multiples the mechanical force applied to another object. With a Type 1 lever, **force** is applied to one end of the lever, and the object to be moved (the **load**) is placed at the other end, with the fulcrum between the two. Varying the distance between the force and the fulcrum and the load and the fulcrum will change the amount of force needed to move the object.

A simple mathematical formula describes this relationship

Work = Force × Distance

Therefore, to lift a unit of weight with the force of half a unit, the distance from the fulcrum to the point where force is applied must be twice the distance between the load and the fulcrum.

Can you cover the text and explain it in your own words? Even though it's describing a very simple machine, you probably found it a bit difficult.

Now, however, look at this diagram:

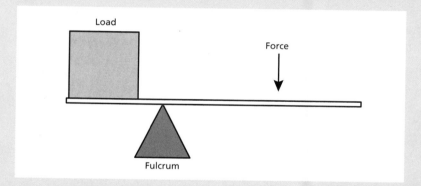

Read the explanation again, this time while looking at the diagram. Then look only at the diagram. Now can you explain what a lever is? Explain it to a partner using the diagram.

Vocabulary

In Unit 2, you learned about word parts and their meanings. One part, suffixes, can help you determine what part of speech a word is—that is, whether it is a noun, verb, adjective, or adverb. Some words can be more than one part of speech (2). Write the words into the appropriate categories in the chart on page 29. Not every box in each row will be filled in, and some boxes may have more than one form. If any words are unfamiliar to you, check their meanings with your instructor or in a dictionary. When you finish, work with a partner to draw conclusions about which suffixes typically identify a certain part of speech.

analogous analogy	diffuse diffusion	produce production
appear appearance	evaporate evaporation	rapid rapidly
atmosphere atmospheric	exist existence	separate (2) separately separation
basic basically	form (2) formation	simple simplify simplistic
create creation	grow growth	type (2) typical typically typify
crystal (2) crystalline crystallize	hexagon hexagonal	universal universally universe
define definition	liquefy liquid	

noun	verb	adjective	adverb

Predict

Work with a partner. Look at the title of the reading (page 31). What do you think the reading will be about? Circle the best answers.

1. how snowflakes are formed

2. what snowflakes look like

3. how to create a snowflake in a laboratory

4. whether two snowflakes can ever be alike

5. how temperature affects the appearance of snowflakes

6. how different languages have a different number of words for "snow"

7. what causes snowstorms

8. why there is rarely thunder or lightening during snowstorms

Skim

Skim the reading (pages 31–33) quickly. Then circle your answers to the questions.

1. The reading will be *easy / medium / difficult* for me to understand.

2. The reading contains *mostly facts / mostly opinions / a mix of facts and opinions.*

3. There are (*three / four / five*) diagrams or illustrations.

Scan

Find the answers to these questions as quickly as you can. Raise your hand to show your instructor when you have finished.

1. At what temperature in Fahrenheit does water freeze? _____

2. At what temperature in Centigrade do water droplets in clouds begin to freeze? _____

3. At what temperature in Fahrenheit do water droplets in clouds begin to freeze? _____

4. What does the word *dendrite* mean?_____

5. How many ways are there to arrange 15 books on a shelf? _____

Read

Read the excerpt from a textbook. For this reading, you may use a dictionary if you like.

The Physics of a Snowflake

1 The basic building block of a snowflake is ice—frozen water. The simplest form of snowflake is a single crystal of frozen water, also known as a snow crystal. However, what most people consider to be a snowflake is actually a conglomeration of snow crystals joined together.

2 Water is formed from one oxygen atom joined to two hydrogen atoms (H_2O). Water exists as a solid (ice), a liquid (water), or a gas (water vapor).

3 In the water cycle, water evaporates (or turns from liquid to vapor) from lakes, rivers, and other sources and rises into the atmosphere. The molecules from water vapor condense, or change to the liquid stage, onto dust particles in the air, forming droplets. Many of these droplets together make up a cloud.

4 Snowflakes are formed when the water molecules in clouds freeze. For this to happen, the droplets in the clouds must be supercooled, meaning they are below the temperature for freezing (0°C / 32°F). At or below temperatures of −10°C (14°F), however, the droplets do begin to freeze. As one droplet freezes, it becomes a snow crystal. Gradually, other droplets will freeze and attach to the snow crystal to form a snowflake.

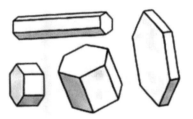

Figure 2.1. A snowflake is a hexagonal prism

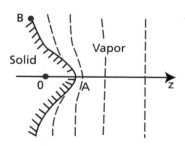

Figure 2.2. Water molecules moving through air

5 The basic shape of a snowflake is a hexagonal prism (see Figure 2.1). These can be plates (flat) or columns (tall). Small snow crystals are usually simple hexagons. As more water molecules attach to these hexagons, the snowflake grows. Water molecules must diffuse through the air, which slows them down. Therefore, they reach any surface of the snowflake that sticks out first and join to that. (See Figure 2.2) This in turn creates a

surface that sticks out more, and more molecules will attach to it, and so forth. This creates the dendrites, or branches, that give the snowflake its lacy appearance. The word *dendrite*, in fact, means "tree like." (See Figure 2.3). As the branches grow, small bumps on each branch also become branches, and so on. This process is known as "branching instability," and

Figure 2.3. Notice the tree-like branches—or dendrites—in these snowflakes.

is a major factor in creating the complex shapes of snowflakes.

6 Many atmospheric conditions affect the growth and shape of a snowflake. Temperature differences combined with different levels of humidity, for example, produce more plates or more columns, as well as influence the occurrence of dendrites. See Figure 2.4 for a graphic representation of the effects of temperature and humidity levels (supersaturation) on snowflake shape.

7 Furthermore, when air pressure is lower, molecules can move more rapidly through the air and reach the facets of a snow crystal more easily; consequently, less branching occurs. At higher air pressure, snowflakes typically develop longer branches.

8 One of the most common questions about snowflakes, after "How are

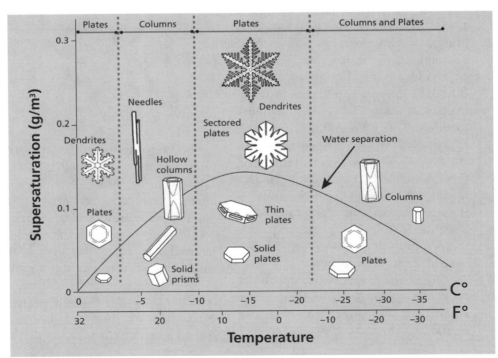

Figure 2.4. How temperature and humidity influence snowflakes

they made?" is, of course, "Is it really true that no two snowflakes are alike?" The answer is both yes and no—depending on your definition of a snowflake. If a snowflake were created from just one water molecule—what would be referred to as a nano-snowflake, or an extremely small one—then yes, it is possible for two snowflakes to be alike, since some water molecules are alike. However, except in laboratory conditions, this is not what we usually mean by a "snowflake."

9 The larger, more complex snowflakes that occur in nature are all different. Consider this analogy: Take 15 different books. How many ways can you arrange them on your bookshelf? There are 15 possible positions for the first book, 14 possible positions for the second book, and so on. If you do the math, you'll find that there are over a trillion (1,000,000,000) ways to arrange just those 15 books. If you had a hundred books, there would be 10^{158} (or, a 1 followed by 158 zeros).

10 A complex snow crystal can have a hundred separate features, each of which could have grown separately—so just as many possibilities as those hundred books. In fact, it's 1,070 times greater than the total number of atoms in the entire universe. That is why we can say with confidence that no two complex snow crystals, not just in any one snowstorm but in fact throughout the history of the earth, have ever looked exactly alike.

Post-Reading Activities

Main Ideas

Write T if the statement is true or F if the statement is false.

1. The main purpose of this passage is to explain how temperature affects the shape of snowflakes. _____

2. Snowflakes form any time that water is falling from clouds and the temperature is below freezing. _____

3. Air pressure affects the appearance of snowflakes. _____

4. Outside of a laboratory, you won't find two snowflakes that look alike. _____

Details

Complete the sentences with words from the box. Two words will not be used.

atom	droplets	humidity
crystal	dust	hydrogen
dendrites	hexagon	snowflake

1. Water is made from one molecule of oxygen and two molecules of _____.

2. A cloud is made up of many _____ of water.

3. Water molecules attach to _____ to form droplets.

4. The very simplest form of a snowflake is a single snow _____.

5. The basic shape of a snowflake is a _____.

6. Both temperature and _____ affect the growth and shape of a snowflake.

7. Snowflakes get their lacy appearance from _____.

Vocabulary

Complete the vocabulary activities with a partner.

1. Find a prefix used in Paragraphs 4 and 6 that means "extra" or "very."

   _____

2. Find a prefix used in Paragraph 8 that means "extremely small."

   _____

3. Find at least one example of each of these kinds of definitions in the text, and on a separate sheet of paper, write the word and the definition. Then compare your examples with another pair. Important terms can be defined by

   • giving the definition after a dash —
   • giving the definition in parentheses ( )
   • using expressions such as *means/meaning, (be) (also) known as*
   • using a form of the *be* verb
   • giving a definition in a phrase starting with *or*

Reading Skills: Understanding and Using Charts and Illustrations

Study the diagrams/illustrations used in the reading. Then follow the directions with a partner.

1. Take turns explaining each diagram or illustration to each other. If necessary, go back and reread the explanation in the text again.

2. Without looking at the diagram or illustration or the text, explain in your own words what causes branching in snowflakes.

Understanding the Text

Circle the best answer. Then discuss your answers with a partner.

1. What kind of audience is this text written for? Why do you think so?
   a. one who knows almost nothing about the subject
   b. one who knows a moderate amount about the subject
   c. one who knows a great deal about the subject

2. Why does the text address the issue of whether two snowflakes can look alike?
   a. It's a common question that people have.
   b. It's easy to explain.
   c. It shows factors affecting the shape of snowflakes.

3. What might the next section of the textbook cover? Circle any reasonable answers.

   a. information about how to stay warm in very cold weather

   b. a discussion of the effects of global warming on traditionally cold areas

   c. a more detailed discussion of factors that affect the shape of snowflakes

   d. an explanation of other types of weather, such as rain, sleet, and fog

   e. a comparison of different types of snow that typically fall in different geographical areas in the world

   f. an explanation of how to create a snow crystal and snowflakes in a laboratory

4. Why does the text use the analogy of arranging books on a bookshelf?

   a. Most people are more interested in books than in snowflakes.

   b. It's an easy example for people to visualize.

   c. There are more books than snowflakes in the world.

   d. After reading a lot about snow, readers will be tired of that subject and want to think about something else.

Extension

Discuss these questions with a small group, or write a paragraph response to each.

1. In what ways is information about how snowflakes are formed useful? What kinds of people would need to know this kind of information?

2. Give some examples of uses of water in its liquid form, its solid form, and its vapor form.

Reading 2: Literature
Pre-Reading Activities

Recognizing Support

A great deal of academic writing involves proving or demonstrating something, whether that is a fact or the writer's opinion. When you write essays or answer essay questions on tests, you will also need to support your opinions.

Support is commonly offered in these ways:

1. an expert's opinion
2. statistics
3. examples or anecdotes (short stories)
4. logical explanations

Writing about literature, poetry, art, and music is especially difficult because it is challenging to support your opinion with "proof." If you are asked to write about another piece of writing, such as a short story, novel, or poem, you will often be asked to provide "support or examples from the text," but it is still up to you to argue convincingly that the examples you've chosen mean what you say they do.

Practice Recognizing Support

Read the following opinions. What kind of support is offered? Number them 1, 2, 3, or 4 according to what type of support they are, as explained in the box. Write 0 if you feel there isn't any support. Then discuss your answers with a partner. Do you think the support is strong or weak?

1. Robert Frost is considered to be one of the greatest American poets. ____

2. Many of the images in Robert Frost's poems are gentle or attractive but still express deep meaning and lessons about life. As Frost himself said, "There are two types of realists: the one who offers a good deal of dirt with his potato to show that it is a real one, and the one who is satisfied with the potato brushed clean. I'm inclined to be the second kind. To me, the thing that art does for life is to clean it, to strip it to form." ____

3. Frost experienced much hardship in his life, in particular through the death of family members. His father died when Robert was 11 years old, and his mother died five years later. His younger sister died in a mental institution in 1929. Four of his six children died before he did, including a daughter who died three days after her birth, a son who died of cholera at age 8, a son who committed suicide as an adult, and a daughter who died in childbirth. ____

4. Robert Frost is a major American poet, having won the Pulitzer Prize for poetry four times. ____

5. Literary students sometimes assume that Robert Frost was a loner, quoting a line from his poem *Mending Wall* that says, "Good fences make good neighbors." However, the line in that poem is spoken by Frost's neighbor, and Frost the poet argues the point in his mind, saying, "' . . . I wonder / If I could put a notion in his head: / 'Why do they make good neighbors? Isn't it / Where there are cows? . . . / Something there is that doesn't love a wall, / That wants it down.'"

____

6. Robert Frost often used snow and ice as images and subjects for his poems because his last name was Frost. ____

7. Robert Frost had that typical New England characteristic of not giving up. When he sold his first poem in 1894 (for $15), he was so proud that he asked his sweetheart Elinor White to marry him. However, she refused because she wanted to finish college. Frost left the area, but returned after she graduated and asked her again, and this time she accepted. ____

8. Robert Frost's most famous poem is *The Road Not Taken*. ____

Vocabulary

Discussing poetry often involves some specific terminology. Read these definitions. Then complete the paragraph with the correct word.

imagery: the use of descriptive language to "paint a picture" for the reader or appeal to other senses such as sound, smell, or taste. This term includes the use of metaphors and symbols described. Imagery often involves *figurative*, or indirect, imaginative language, as opposed to *literal* language that has a very direct meaning.

metaphor: a comparison between two seemingly unlike objects or ideas. In the phrase "surf the Internet," for example, the Internet is being compared to the ocean. Sometimes the metaphor is made directly, using *like* or *as*. This particular type is called a *simile*: "The Internet is like an ocean of knowledge."

rhyme: when the final one or two syllables of two words have the same sound. For example, *moon*, *spoon*, and *June* rhyme.

rhyme scheme: the pattern of rhyming. For example, rhyming the last word of every line of a poem, or the last word of every other line of a poem, are rhyme schemes.

setting: the place (and sometimes time) where action in the poem is happening. It could be a country, or a house, or an outdoor area.

stanza: a group of lines in a poem, similar to a verse in a song.

symbol: something (a word or idea) that represents something else. For example, a poet might write about plants growing in the springtime as a symbol for birth and leaves falling in the autumn as a symbol for death. Look at these ways to talk about symbols:

The falling leaves **are a symbol** for death.

The falling leaves **represent** death.

The falling leaves **symbolize** death.

An Analysis of *Good Hours*

Robert Frost frequently used the ① _____ of his native New England in his poems to create visuals for his readers. In fact, one of his earlier collections of poems was called *North of Boston*. His ② _____ is often calm and simple, and he writes about ordinary things and people. For example, this is the first ③ _____ of his 1915 poem *Good Hours*:

> I had for my winter evening walk—
> No one at all with whom to talk,
> But I had the cottages in a row
> Up to their shining eyes in snow.

The lines are short, with a simple ④ _____ of aabb (the first two lines ⑤ _____, and then the second two lines do). The literal meaning of the words is not hard to understand: the poet has gone for a walk alone, but doesn't feel lonely. The houses are used as a ⑥ _____ for a human face (*their shining eyes*).

However, the poem works on several levels. In the third stanza, Frost writes:

> I had such company outward bound.
> I went till there were no cottages found.
> I turned and repented, but coming back
> I saw no window but that was black.

Frost's simple walk through the village is also a ⑦ _____ for man's journey through life. In the poem, Frost talks about leaving behind the company of children in the second stanza:

> I had a glimpse through curtain laces
> Of youthful forms and youthful faces

In the third stanza, he talks about turning to look back; however, he cannot go back and find things the way they were. In the final stanza, his lines

> Over the snow my creaking feet
> Disturbed the slumbering village street

sound like an old man ready to depart life, leaving the village for those still young and living.

Predict

Predicting is a more challenging skill for literature, especially poetry. However, you can prepare for some of the themes of Frost's poetry in this unit. Discuss these questions with a small group.

1. What are some things that snow or ice might symbolize in a poem? Do you think snow would usually represent something positive or something negative, or is there no general pattern?

2. What are some things that a forest might symbolize in a poem?

3. Do you think of these emotions as "hot" or "cold"? Answer without thinking too much; just give your first impression.
   - anger
   - fear
   - happiness
   - hate
   - jealousy
   - joy
   - loneliness
   - love

Skim

Skimming and scanning are not usually used with literature except to get a sense of the type or how long the reading is. Skim the reading (pages 42–44) quickly to see the types and length. Then answer the questions.

1. How many poems are there? _____

2. What other type of texts are there in addition to the poems? _____

_____

Read

Read both poems that are part of a test. Then read the essay questions on the test and answers about them. Use a dictionary if you like.

Stopping By Woods on a Snowy Evening (1923)

Whose woods these are I think I know.
His house is in the village though;
He will not see me stopping here
To watch his woods fill up with snow.

My little horse must think it queer
To stop without a farmhouse near
Between the woods and frozen lake
The darkest evening of the year.

He gives his harness bells a shake
To ask if there is some mistake.
The only other sound's the sweep
Of easy wind and downy flake.

The woods are lovely, dark and deep.
But I have promises to keep,
And miles to go before I sleep,
And miles to go before I sleep.

Dust of Snow (1923)

The way a crow
Shook down on me
The dust of snow
From a hemlock tree

Has given my heart
A change of mood
And saved some part
Of a day I had rued.

English 102
Sebastian Mitchell
April 11, 2010

Essay Question 1 (25 points)

Analyze the setting in _Stopping by Woods on a Snowy Evening_. Use phrases from the poem to support your analysis.

1. Robert Frost uses the setting of "Stopping by Woods on a Snowy Evening" in two ways. The first is literal; that is, as an actual snowy forest. Although a dark, cold forest can symbolize hardship or suffering, the mood of this setting is not gloomy. Rather, it is peaceful. Frost talks of "easy wind and downy flake." "Downy" means "soft and gentle," suggesting that the snow is only a harmless powder. Frost is using the snow as a symbol of beauty. The same can be inferred about the darkness, which is the expected darkness of nightfall and is not unnatural. In the final stanza, Frost calls the darkness "lovely." The "darkest evening of the year" could be December 21, the shortest day of the year. The rider would need to hurry on to his home or wherever he has to go because it is more difficult to ride at night and he still has "miles to go."

However, the setting can also be seen in a metaphorical way. The man in the poem is traveling on a road "Between the woods and frozen lake," a road that can represent the journey of life. On his journey, the man stops at a particular location that is filling up with snow. Snow in its true nature is cleansing as it covers up trash and ugliness, and obscuring as it hides obstacles. This blanket of beauty catches the man's attention for a while, but in the end he remembers that he has "promises to keep" and continues along his path. The horse, who has no higher purpose in life, is confused by the stop; it is the man who is distracted from his purpose by visual beauty.

Frost reminds us to pause during the journey of our lives to enjoy moments of quiet beauty, but not to let the snow of distraction prevent us from keeping our promises.

Essay Question 2 (20 points)

Discuss the imagery of snow in *Dust of Snow*. How does it affect the mood of the poem?

2. Snow is often used in poetry to symbolize negative or dark ideas, such as cold feelings, the lack of emotion, or even death. However, Robert Frost uses snow in a very different way in his 1923 poem "Dust of Snow."

The very title of the poem suggests a light, almost frivolous use of snow because of the word "dust." We think of dust as something without weight, much lighter than real snow, and of no importance.

We know that the poet had been feeling sad or upset before because he mentions "a day I had rued," or regretted, but by the end of the poem, the poet seems to have brightened up a bit. It might be that the crow had startled him and in his moment of surprise, the man realized the trouble in his day was over. Perhaps the notion that a small thing such as a crow could affect him in a big way cheered him. Maybe the man was so caught up in the ridiculousness and unexpectedness of the moment that he forgot about the previous troubles of the day. Whatever the case, Frost shows us that even the most frivolous of things can impact us in a big way if we take the time to notice them.

Post-Reading Activities

Main Ideas

Circle the best answer.

Stopping by Woods on a Snowy Evening

1. How many possible meanings for the setting are given by the essay writer?

   a. one

   b. two

   c. three

2. What does the essay writer think the mood of the setting is?

   a. positive

   b. negative

   c. neutral

3. What is the most important meaning of the poem?

   a. literal

   b. metaphorical

   c. Answers a and b are equally important.

4. What does the essay writer think that Frost wants the readers to do?

   a. move through their lives more slowly

   b. sometimes stop and relax, but not for too long

   c. not be distracted from the true purpose of their lives

5. How can the rhyme scheme be represented?

   a. aabb; ccdd; eeff; gggg

   b. aaba; ccdc; eefe; gggg

   c. aaba; bbcb; ccdc; dddd

Dust of Snow

6. What meaning does the essay writer believe that snow has in this poem?

   a. positive

   b. negative

   c. neutral

7. How many possible reasons why the man's mood could have changed are given by the essay writer?

   a. three

   b. four

   c. five

8. What does the essay writer believe that Frost wants readers to do?

   a. not regret any of their actions

   b. spend more time outdoors

   c. appreciate small or trivial things

9. How can the rhyme scheme be represented?

   a. abba; baab

   b. abab; cdcd

   c. abab; baba

Reading Skills: Recognizing Support

Answer the questions with a partner.

1. What kinds of support does the writer use in the essays? Check (✓) all that apply.

   ____ information from class discussions

   ____ quotations from professors who have studied Frost

   ____ lines from the poem

   ____ the writer's own impressions and ideas

   ____ information from Frost talking about his poem

2. How many direct quotes from the poem does the writer use in the first essay? _____
   in the second? _____

3. Do you think the writer used enough support? Why or why not? What additional support could be added to the essays?

Vocabulary

Read the poems again. Then fill in the blanks.

1. Write the words from the first poem that are synonyms for these words:

   a. town _____

   b. strange _____

   c. iced _____

   d. movement _____

   e. blowing _____

   f. soft _____

2. Write the words from the second poem that are synonyms for these words:

   a. dropped; pushed _____

   b. evergreen _____

   c. feeling _____

   d. regretted _____

Extension

Discuss these questions with a partner or a small group, or write a paragraph response for each.

1. What does this quotation by Robert Frost mean? Do you agree or disagree?

   "A poem begins in delight and ends in wisdom."

2. Should poetry and literature be studied by all high school students? By all university students? Why or why not?

3. Should a poet who wants to use snow as a symbol or image in poetry understand the physics of a snowflake? Why or why not?

4. Read the two poems by Robert Frost. Then choose one of the essay questions. Discuss the question with another group that has chosen the same poem. Then write your answer to the question.

Fire and Ice (1923)

Some say the world will end in fire,
Some say in ice.
From what I've tasted of desire
I hold with those who favour fire.
But if it had to perish twice,
I think I know enough of hate
To say that for destruction ice
Is also great
And would suffice.

A Patch of Old Snow (1916)

There's a patch of old snow in a corner
That I should have guessed
Was a blow-away paper the rain
Had brought to rest.

It is speckled with grime as if
Small print overspread it,
The news of a day I've forgotten—
If I ever read it.

Essay Question 1:
Explain the metaphors and symbols in *Fire and Ice*. Do you think they are accurate?

Essay Question 2:
What does the snow represent in *A Patch of Old Snow*? What message is Frost trying to convey to his readers?

Hair

Discuss

Discuss these questions with a small group.

1. Describe your hair care routine during a typical week. How do you choose your hair care products? How do you dry your hair? Do you style it in any special way?

2. Read the topics that may be covered in college textbooks. In which university classes might you read about each? Choose subject areas from the box or add your own ideas. More than one answer is possible.

anthropology	chemistry	history	sociology
art	English	linguistics	theater
biology	environmental studies		

a. differences between men's and women's hairstyles during the 1800s in England _____

b. the process used to determine someone's DNA from a strand of hair

_____

c. origins and explanations for idioms in English with the word *hair* (*a hair's breadth; to split hairs; get out of one's hair; make one's hair stand on end; not a hair out of place*) _____

d. how to test for arsenic and other poisons using someone's hair

_____

e. explanation of painting hair using watercolors _____

f. causes of hair loss _____

g. hair-cutting rituals in three African countries_____

h. the process used to determine what color hair a child will be born with _____

3. Which of these factors do you think determines whether your hair is straight, curly, or wavy? Explain your guesses.

___ what your parents' hair looked like

___ what your grandparents' hair looked like

___ where you were born

___ how old you are

___ what you eat

___ what kind of shampoo you use

Reading 1: Chemistry

Pre-Reading Activities

Dictionary Skills 1: Pronunciation

In academic reading, you will encounter new vocabulary. However, not all new vocabulary is of equal importance to you. As you become a more efficient reader, you will begin to classify new vocabulary. Start by asking questions when you encounter a new word.

Question: Do I need to know what it means?

Answer: No = Skip over it.

Yes = Look it up in a dictionary or guess the meaning from context. Then ask yourself the next question.

Question: Do I need to remember it?

Answer: No = Don't write it.

Yes = Use appropriate strategies to memorize it.

Of course, there are different levels of "remembering" a word. Do you need to just recognize it when you see it again? Or will you need to be able to write it on a test, either as a single word or used correctly in a sentence?

This unit focuses on remembering key words that you would need to be able to use on a test. One good way to remember new vocabulary words is to be able to pronounce them.

Even native English speakers can't always guess how to pronounce English words when they read them. To learn a word's pronunciation (if you can't ask your instructor because you are reading outside of class), look up the word in the dictionary.

Different dictionaries can have different symbols to explain pronunciation. A key or guide to the pronunciation symbols should be in the front of your dictionary. This shows how vowels are pronounced and also shows syllable stress; that is, which part of the word gets the most emphasis. This is not something you can always guess from just reading a word.

If you cannot easily remember your dictionary's way of showing a word's pronunciation, it's a good idea to invent your own way to make sure you accurately pronounce the word later.

Practice saying new words out loud. Use them in class discussions if you can; if that's not possible, say them out loud alone in your room. This will help you remember them. In addition, spelling them out loud and writing them will help you be able to write them on a test.

Vocabulary

Look at the diagrams. Make sure you can pronounce each word. Check a dictionary for pronunciation of any new words. You can check with your instructor later, but use your dictionary first.

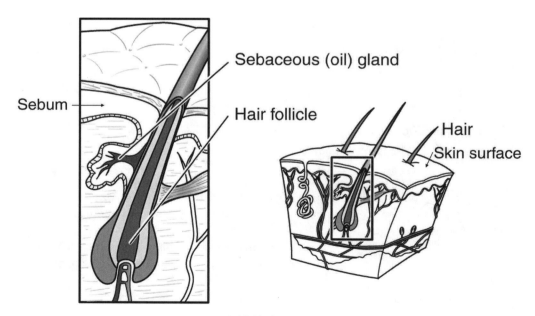

Hair follicle anatomy

Predict

Work with a partner. Read the title of the reading (page 54). What do you think the reading will be about? What do you think are some purposes of the ingredients in shampoo?

Skim

Skim the reading (pages 54–56) quickly. Then circle your answers to the questions.

1. The reading will be *easy / medium / difficult* for me to understand.

2. The reading contains *a lot of / some / very few* scientific terms.

3. The reading contains *mostly facts / mostly opinions / a mix of facts and opinions*.

Scan

Find the answers to these questions as quickly as you can. Raise your hand to show your instructor when you have finished.

1. How many diagrams or illustrations are there? _____

2. What is the pH of pure water? _____

3, How many types of surfactants are there? _____

4, What are the different types of surfactants? _____

5. What is the name of one ingredient in shampoos that affects clarity? _____

Read

Read the excerpt from a textbook. Imagine that the underlined words are words that you will need to know for a test later. You can decide if you want to look them up as you read or after you finish.

What's in Your Shampoo?

1 What makes hair dirty? And what cleans it? Normal hair gets coated with <u>sebum</u>, a type of thick oil. Sebum protects hair from sun, air, and water by coating the hair follicle. However, particles of dust and dirt, flakes of skin from the scalp, and even excess conditioner can stick to the sebum. This combination is what people feel when they say their hair is "dirty."

2 Soap and shampoo remove the sebum and the dirt and skin attached to the sebum. Soap, however, removes too much sebum from the hair and leaves it dry and unprotected. Harsh shampoos can do this too.

3 Healthy hair has a <u>hydrophobic</u> surface; that is, water doesn't stick to it, but oil (such as sebum) does. Therefore, just rinsing your hair with water doesn't remove the sebum and dirt. Shampoo uses a <u>surfactant</u>, a foaming and cleaning agent, whose molecule has a <u>hydrophilic</u> "head" and a hydrophobic "tail" (see Figure 3.1). The hydrophilic head attaches to water, and the hydrophobic tail attaches to the sebum, so the oils and dirt can be washed away in water (see Figure 3.2).

4 One reason that shampoo makers typically advertise that their shampoos are "pH balanced" is because of the need to smooth hair that has been stripped of its sebum. When sebum is removed, the scales on the hair cuticle become dull and rough. A pH (acid/alkaline balance) of around 5.5 to 6.5 restores acidity to the hair, and smoothes the cuticle. This is one reason that rinsing hair in regular household vinegar will leave it feeling especially soft; it's also why citric acid or lemon juice is commonly added to shampoos. You remember from Chapter 1 that pure water has a pH balance of 7; below that is considered acid, and above it alkaline.

5 There are four main types of surfactants used in shampoos. Their chemical makeup and properties will be described in more detail in the next

Hydrophobic Group
"Fat Loving End"

Hydrophilic Group
"Water Loving Head"

Figure 3.1 A surfactant molecule

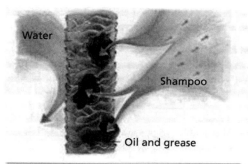
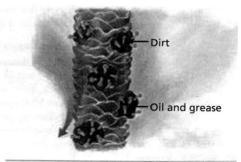

A. The tail of the shampoo molecule is attracted to oil and dirt.

B. Shampoo causes oils to roll up into small globules.

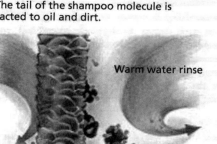
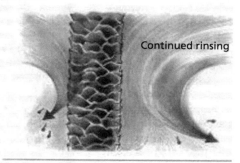

C. During rinsing, the heads of the shampoo molecules attach to water molecules and causes debris to roll off.

D. Thorough rinsing washes away debris and excess shampoo.

Figure 3.2 The cleaning process

chapter. Surfactants can be <u>anionic</u>, <u>cationic</u>, <u>amphoteric</u>, or <u>nonionic</u>. Often shampoos will combine two or more of these in what the industry calls a "shampoo system."

6 Common anionics include sodium (or ammonium) laureth sulfate and sodium (or ammonium) lauryl sulfate. These ingredients are often listed first, as they are the primary cleansing agents in the shampoo. Some people find these to be too drying for hair, and in particular for curly hair.

7 Cationics provide a bit more conditioning for hair, and also can improve the <u>viscosity</u> of the shampoo formula. Some commonly used cationics include olealkonium chloride, distearyldimonium chloride, and isostearyl ethyldimonium ethosulfate.

8 The main purpose of amphoterics is to provide a better texture for the shampoo and its lather. Cocamidopropyl betaine and cocamidopropyl hydroxysultaine are examples of this kind of surfactant.

9 Nonionics such as polyethylene glycol (PEG)-150 distearate and cocamide MEA also are primarily used to affect viscosity and lather. PEG-80 sorbitan laurate also cleanses.

10 Of course, these days most people expect more from their shampoo than simple cleansing.

They may want the formula to condition their hair, leave it softer, or protect it from ultraviolet rays from the sun. They may want a particular scent or color. Shampoo formulators also add ingredients to affect the shampoo's color and appearance. Below are some properties of shampoo and common additives used to achieve them. Consider which properties are desirable to you before beginning the Shampoo Formulation Lab in section 3.6.

Clarity: ethyl alcohol; glycerol; sodium xylene sulfonate

Opaqueness: glycol distearate; different types of resin latex

Pearlescence: glycol stearate; glycol distearate

Thickness: cocamide monoisopropanolamide; sodium chloride; sodium citrate

Conditioning: dimethicone; stear-alkonium chloride; a variety of quaternized cellulosic polymers such as quaternium-5 or quaternium-18

11 Finally, shampoo formulators have to consider such things as how well all the ingredients work with each other. Often preservatives are added to keep the shampoo looking, smelling, and working in the same way over a long period of time.

Post-Reading Activities

Main Ideas

Circle the answer that best expresses the main ideas of the reading.

1. What is the main purpose of the reading?
    a. to prepare students for a laboratory assignment
    b. to argue that not all shampoo ingredients are necessary
    c. to explain the main types of ingredients in shampoos

2. Why does hair get dirty?
    a. Dust and other things stick to oil on the hair.
    b. Dirt gets transferred to hair when people touch it.
    c. People don't wash their hair with the right kind of shampoo.

3. Why can't you use just water to clean your hair?
    a. Water doesn't stick to the surface of hair.
    b. It won't leave your hair soft enough.
    c. You can, but advertisers want to sell you shampoo.

4. What is a surfactant?
    a. part of the hair follicle
    b. a type of oil
    c. something that cleans hair

5. How many main types of surfactants are there?
    a. three
    b. four
    c. five

6. What do amphoterics do?
    a. make a shampoo formula feel better
    b. make a shampoo formula look better
    c. make a shampoo formula smell better

Details

Read the statements. Write T if the statement is true and F if the statement is false.

1. Vinegar and lemon juice can be used to make hair feel soft. _____

2. Sodium lauryl sulfate is a good choice for people with curly hair. _____

3. Distearyldimonium chloride is an example of a cationic. _____

4. Cocamidopropyl betaine and cocamidopropl hydroxysultaine are used primarily for cleaning. _____

5. One type of a nonionic is cocamide MEA. _____

6. Shampoo makers also consider factors such as color, scent, and appearance. _____

7. Glycerol affects pearlescence. _____

8. Cocamide monoisopropanolamide is used for conditioning. _____

9. Sodium xylene sulfonate and quaternium-5 are used for the same purpose. _____

10. Preservatives are used to help the qualities of shampoo formulas last longer. _____

Work with a partner. Change each false statement so it is true in two different ways. One has been done for you as an example.

2. Sodium lauryl sulfate isn't a good choice for people with curly hair.

    Sodium lauryl sulfate can be too drying for curly hair.

    _____

    _____

    _____

    _____

    _____

    _____

    _____

Reading Skills: Dictionary Skills: Pronunciation

Answer the questions with a partner.

1. Do you know how to pronounce the underlined words in the reading? Make notes about the pronunciation of these words so that you can remember how to say them. Make sure you and your partner pronounce the words the same way. Then explain your system to another pair.

   Next look at these additional words from the reading.

   a. conditioner _____

   b. molecule _____

   c. pH _____

   d. isostearyl ethyldimonium ethosulfate _____

   e. pearlescence _____

2. Is it important to know how to pronounce the words listed in Question 1? Why or why not?

   _____

   _____

   _____

3. How long would it take you to memorize the underlined words so that you could write them on a test? How would you memorize them? Make a list, and then discuss different techniques.

   _____

   _____

   _____

4. Imagine you had to memorize the chemicals that affect the thickness of a shampoo (including the spelling of those words). How would you do it? Make a list, and then discuss different techniques.

   _____

   _____

   _____

Understanding the Text

Answer the questions about the reading.

1. What are students going to do after reading this section of their textbook? Circle all correct answers.

   a. create their own shampoo in a laboratory

   b. analyze samples of shampoos to see what their ingredients are

   c. learn more about the chemical structures of shampoo ingredients

   d. make their own conditioner

   e. analyze what is in the shampoos they use at home

2. *Cationic, anionic,* and *nonionic* all share the root *ion*, meaning "a particle that is electrically charged." How would you remember the meaning of these words using this information? Compare your strategies with those of a partner.

   cation = positively charged ion _____

   anion = negatively charged ion _____

   nonionic = having no electrical charge _____

3. Imagine that you have checked the ingredients on a bottle of shampoo and found this chemical listed: polyquaternium-10. What do you think its function is? Why do you think so?

   _____

   _____

   _____

   _____

Extension

Discuss these questions with a partner or a small group, or write a paragraph response for each.

1. Copy the ingredients from the shampoo you use most often, and bring the list to class. Work with a group to determine what the functions of the ingredients are. How many could you definitely identify? How many could you make a good guess about? How many were you unable to identify at all?

2. Imagine you are talking to someone with no background in chemistry. Explain in your own words how shampoo works.

Reading 2: Genetics

Pre-Reading Activities

Using Word Parts

Understanding the basic meaning of word roots, prefixes, and suffixes can sometimes help you figure out the meaning of a new word—but you might still need to check your guess in a dictionary.

However, knowing the meanings of different word parts is also a great help in remembering what words mean after you've looked them up, especially if you are trying to remember the difference between two similar words.

For example, if you know that *hydro* means *water*, *phil-* or *philo-* means *love*, and *phobo-* or *phobi-* means *hate*, then you can guess a little bit at the meaning of the words *hydrophilic* and *hydrophobic*. Now, "water love" or "water hate" isn't enough for you to really understand the meaning of the word. However, after you have checked the words in your dictionary, it will be easy for you to remember which kind of molecule, hydrophilic or hydrophobic, attracts water and which repels water.

When you read new vocabulary words that you will need to remember for tests, especially in the sciences, be sure to notice in your dictionary if they are made up of roots, prefixes, and suffixes that have a meaning. Write these meanings too, in addition to the meaning of the entire word and its pronunciation.

English is made up of many, many words parts from several different languages. It isn't efficient to try to learn them all. However, knowing some common ones can be very useful for you, and over time, you will learn the ones that are most common in your field of study.

Vocabulary

Match the word roots, prefixes, and suffixes used in the reading on the left with their meanings on the right. Use a dictionary if necessary.

1. **hetero–** _____   a. same
2. **homo–** _____   b. showing
3. **gen–** _____   c. master; in charge
4. **geno–** _____   d. kind of
5. **pheno–** _____   e. joined together; union
6. **domin–** _____   f. different
7. **–cess–** _____   g. race (as of people); kind of
8. **–type** _____   h. move, yield, go, surrender
9. **alle–** _____   i. other
10. **zyg–, zygo–** _____   j. to produce or become

Predict

Work with a partner and study the additional vocabulary. Then look at the title of the reading, and read the *Looking Ahead* paragraph on page 64. Use your dictionary to understand any new words if necessary. Which of the following do you think will be covered in the reading? Check (✓) your guesses.

Additional Vocabulary
organism: a living thing that has or will develop the ability to function independently
offspring: children; descendents; new organisms produced by parents
traits: features or characteristics passed on from parents to offspring

___ an explanation of the difference between curly and wavy hair

___ an explanation of what hair types offspring inherit from their parents

___ a discussion of the importance of distinguishing different hair types

___ exercises to figure out what traits will be inherited by offspring

___ a discussion of hair colors and how they're inherited

Skim

Skim the reading (pages 64–66) quickly. Then answer the questions.

1. The reading will be *easy / medium / difficult* for me to understand.

2. The charts *are necessary / are not necessary* to understand the reading.

3. Find the title, the headings, and the bold vocabulary words. Write a question for each one, such as *What does ___ mean,* or *What is the difference between ___ and ___ ,* or *What is/are ___ used for?*

   a. _____

   b. _____

   c. _____

   d. _____

   e. _____

   f. _____

   g. _____

   h. _____

   i. _____

   j. _____

Scan

Find the answers to these questions as quickly as you can. Raise your hand to show your instructor when you have finished.

1. What is the name of the type of diagrams shown on pages 65–66? _____

2. What type of organism is mentioned during the discussion of tallness and shortness? _____

3. What type of organism is mentioned during the discussion of straight, wavy, and curly hair? _____

Read

Read the excerpt from a textbook. For this reading, do not use a dictionary. Underline any words that you do not understand.

3.6: Different Patterns of Heredity

1 *Looking Ahead:* What type of hair do you have? Curly? Wavy? Straight? How about your parents? Your grandparents? In this section, you will learn how to predict traits in offspring when the patterns of heredity are more complex than the simple dominant or recessive patterns studied in section 3.5.

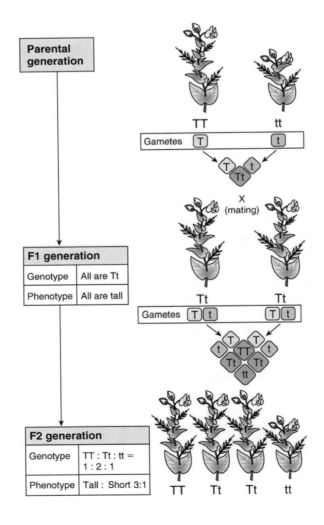

Review from 3.5:
- Gregor Mendel (1822–1844), the "father of genetics," used pea plants to show that traits were inherited in predictable patterns.
- **Genes**, located on **chromosomes**, exist in alternative forms called **alleles**. For example the difference between a tall and a short pea plant is determined by the alleles for tallness and shortness. A pea plant could have two alleles for tallness, TT (**homozygous**); two alleles for shortness, tt (homozygous); or one allele for tallness and one allele for shortness, Tt (**heterozygous**).
- The way an organism looks is its **phenotype**. A pea heterozygous pea plant's phenotype is tall, because the plant looks tall. The **genotype** expresses the gene combination of an organism. A heterozygous pea plant has the genotype Tt.
- In cases of **complete dominance**, a **dominant** gene overrules a **recessive** gene. For example, since tallness is dominant over shortness in pea plants, if a pea plant has one allele for tallness and one for shortness, the plant will present as tall.
- **Offspring** receive one copy of each chromosome from the female parent and one copy from the male parent.

Punnett Squares

2 A Punnett square is a type of graphical representation used to predict the outcome of a cross between two parent organisms. It was named for British biologist Reginald Punnett, who devised the technique in 1905.

3 A Punnett square that shows the possible results of a cross between two heterozygous tall pea plants follows. Remember that each heterozygous parent has one allele for tallness and one allele for shortness, and that each parent passes on one allele to the next generation.

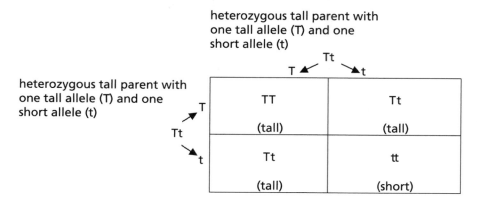

4 Since we know that tallness (T) is dominant over shortness (t), we know that a TT plant has the phenotype tall, a Tt plant has the phenotype tall, and a tt plant has the phenotype short. Therefore, if two heterozygous pea plants are bred together, there is a 75 percent chance that their offspring will have the phenotype tall.

Incomplete Dominance

5 When inheritance follows a pattern of complete dominance, then both heterozygous and homozygous individuals with the dominant gene will have the same phenotype. However, in cases of incomplete dominance, there is a new phenotype created for a heterozygous combination. As an example, we will examine the presence of curly and straight hair in humans.

6 Homozygous straight hair has the genotype SS. Homozygous curly hair has the genotype CC. However, heterozygous hair SC does not have either the phenotype straight or the phenotype curly, but rather wavy. Look at the Punnett square.

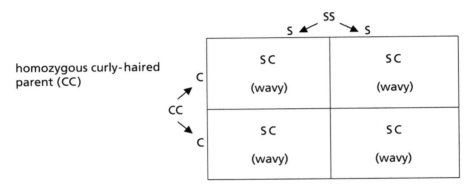

7 All of the children born to these parents would have wavy hair. Now look at what happens when a heterozygous wavy-haired person has a child with a homozygous curly-haired person.

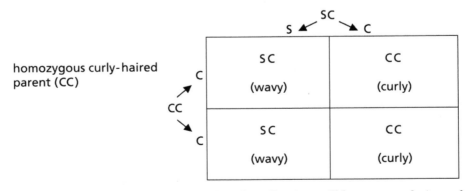

8 There is a 50 percent chance that the offspring will have wavy hair, and a 50 percent chance that the offspring will have curly hair. The same would hold true if a heterozygous wavy-haired person had a child with homozygous straight-haired person; that is, there is a 50 percent chance that the child would have straight hair.

Post-Reading Activities

Main Ideas

Circle the answer that best expresses the main ideas of the reading.

1. What is the main purpose of the reading?
    a. to show how heredity in humans and plants is similar
    b. to give an explanation of a certain pattern of heredity
    c. to demonstrate the usefulness of Punnett squares
    d. to discuss applications of theories of genetics

2. What does incomplete dominance mean?
    a. Heterozygous presentations will always look different from homozygous presentations.
    b. Two parent organisms are unable to have offspring.
    c. The genetics of an organism cannot be determined by looking at it.
    d. It isn't possible to determine what offspring of two heterozygous parents will look like.

3. Complete the Punnett square for two wavy-haired parents. Use it to answer the question:
    a. What percentage of children will have straight hair?   _____
    b. What percentage of children will have wavy hair?   _____
    c. What percentage of children will have curly hair?   _____

wavy-haired parent (SC)

SC
S ◄— —► C

wavy-haired parent (SC)   S

SC

C

Details

Fill in the blanks with information learned from the reading to complete true sentences.

1. Punnett squares have been used since _____.

2. A pea plant with Tt alleles would look _____.

3. If two heterozygous tall pea plants are crossed, there is a _____ chance that the offspring will be short.

4. If a wavy-haired person had a child with straight-haired person, their children could either have _____ hair or _____ hair.

Vocabulary

Write answers to the questions. Then discuss them with a partner.

1. Answer the questions that you wrote for the Skim exercise on page 63. Can you pronounce all of the bold vocabulary?

2. Did you underline any words to look up? If so, look them up now. Write the words and their definitions.

_____

_____

_____

3. Now read the article again. Were the words you chose to look up important to understand the reading? Do you wish you had chosen any different words?

_____

_____

_____

Reading Skills: Using Word Parts

Write answers to the questions. Then discuss them with a partner.

1. What is the difference between a *heterozygous* trait and a *homozygous* trait? How can you use your understanding of word parts to remember this difference?

   _____

   _____

2. What is the difference between a *phenotype* and a *genotype*? How can you use your understanding of word parts to remember this difference?

   _____

   _____

3. What is the difference between a *dominant* trait and a *recessive* trait? How can you use your understanding of word parts to remember this difference?

   _____

   _____

Understanding the Text

Circle the best answer.

1. Why did the textbook use pea plants as an example?
   a. Gregor Mendel also used pea plants.
   b. Many people are interested in pea plants.
   c. Pea plants are common.

2. Why did the textbook use hair textures as an example?
   a. Gregor Mendel also studied hair.
   b. Students will be familiar with the appearance of different hair types.
   c. Hair traits are easier to understand than pea plant traits.

Extension

Answer the questions on pages 70–72. Then discuss them with a partner.

1. Draw a Punnett square to determine what the offspring of a homozygous tall pea plant and a heterozygous tall pea plant would look like.

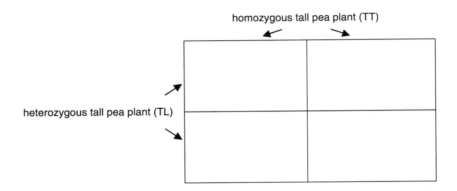

a. What percentage would look tall?_____

b. What percentage would look short?_____

2. Red snapdragons have the alleles RR, and white snapdragons have the alleles WW. A RW combination produces a pink snapdragon. Draw a Punnett square to show what the offspring of a red snapdragon and a white snapdragon would look like.

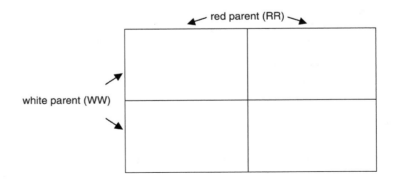

a. What percentage would be red?_____

b. What percentage would be white?_____

c. What percentage would be pink? _____

Now draw a Punnett square to show what the offspring of two pink snapdragons would look like.

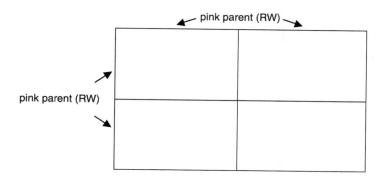

a. What percentage would be red?_____

b. What percentage would be white?_____

c. What percentage would be pink? _____

3. Look at the word parts from the vocabulary in Reading 1. Can you
   guess their meanings? Write the meanings from the box by the correct
   word part. Use a dictionary if necessary.

beyond, excessive	on top of
enter, to go in	together
face or side of something	two by two
first	

a. Shampoo uses a *surfactant*, a foaming and cleaning agent, whose
   molecule has a hydrophilic "head" and a hydrophobic "tail."

   sur = _____

   fac = _____

b. These ingredients are often listed first, as they are the *primary*
   cleansing agents in the shampoo.

   pri = _____

c. They may want the formula to condition their hair, leave it softer,
   or protect it from *ultraviolet* rays from the sun.

   ultra = _____

d. . . .particles of dust and dirt, flakes of skin from the scalp, and even
   excess conditioner can stick to the sebum. This *combination* is what
   people say when they say their hair is "dirty."

   com = _____

   bin = _____

e. Shampoo formulators also add ingredients to affect the shampoo's
   color and appearance.

   ingredi = _____

4

Plastic

Discuss

The activity appears on page 75.

Reading 1: Bio-Engineering
Pre-Reading Activities

Identifying Informed Opinions

To review, facts are pieces of information that can be verified or proved; something known to have happened or existed. Opinions are personal judgments or beliefs that cannot be proved.

At first, it might seem easy to distinguish fact from opinion.

Opinion: *Chocolate is the most delicious flavor.*

Fact: *Chocolate is made from the seeds of the cacao tree.*

The difficulty comes when statements are presented as facts, but you don't have a way to verify if they are true. For example, you might not know if the following statement is true, but you could easily check it.

Fact: *The Ivory Coast is the world's largest exporter of cacao.*

But how about the following statement?

Large single-crop plantations of crops such as cacao trees create an unstable market for local farmers and also significantly damage the local environment.

You could research the background, but you might come to a different conclusion. Therefore, it is really more of an informed opinion; something that can be supported and could be true, but also could be argued. When you read supported opinions, you need to think critically about two things:

1. whether you believe these opinions and why
2. how those opinions could be proved or disproved

Work alone. Mark each statement F for fact, O for opinion, or IO for informed opinion. Then share your answers with a partner or small group. Discuss any differences of opinion, and share ideas about how informed opinions could be checked.

1. At the grocery store, it's better to use plastic bags than paper bags because plastic bags are lighter, stronger, and reusable. _____

2. There are two types of plastics: *thermoplastics*, which will soften and melt if enough heat is applied, and *thermosets*, which will not soften or melt no matter how much heat is applied. _____

3. Manufacturing plastic causes air pollution. _____

4. The first commercially successful type of plastic, Bakelite, was invented in 1907. _____

5. The main reason that plastic garbage is such a problem is that so much plastic is used for product packaging. _____

6. Plastic window frames are not as attractive as wooden ones. _____

7. It's difficult to recycle plastic because there are so many different types. _____

8. Polyethylene terephthalate (PET or PETE), developed in 1941, is used for synthetic fibers in fabrics such as polyester as well as containers for carbonated drinks and fruit juices. _____

9. The advantages of using plastic for many household building materials outweigh the disadvantages. _____

10. Because plastic is made from petroleum, it is important that we find substitutes for plastic as quickly as possible. _____

Vocabulary

Match the word on the left with its definition on the right.

1. biodegrade   a. an arm or leg

2. cartilage   b. a tube that carries blood

3. cast   c. to force a fluid into

4. fracture   d. a hard mold used to hold something still

5. inject   e. a liquid

6. limb   f. to break down from biology

7. solution   g. tissue in the body

8. vessel   h. a break or crack

Study the list of prefixes and suffixes related to the medical words in the reading. Refer to this list after you read the definitions in the reading or check the meanings in your dictionary.

a. **allo–** = different from the normal; other

b. **auto–** = self

c. **bio–** = life

d. **–blast** = bud or germ (in the sense of something that will grow)

e. **chondro–** = cartilage

f. **–clast** = break or destroy

g. **fibro–** = related to *fiber*, a long, threadlike cell

h. **–graft** = to cause two different things to grow together

i. **hema–** = blood

j. **osteo–** = bone

k. **–toma** = cut or incision

Predict

Answer the questions, and then discuss them with a partner.

1. Look at the title of the reading (page 79). Do you think it will contain mostly facts, mostly opinions, mostly informed opinions, or a mix?

   _____

2. What do you think the reading will be about?
   a. making new "bones" for people out of plastic
   b. using plastic inside the body to help people grow new bone
   c. using plastic outside the body to protect it while it is growing new bone inside

Skim

Skim the reading (pages 79–80) quickly. Then circle your answers to the questions.

1. The reading will be *easy / medium / difficult* for me to understand.

2. The reading is about *something being used in hospitals now / something still being developed*.

3. The reading mainly discusses *blood diseases / broken bones / elderly patients*.

4. The reading *contains / does not contain* interviews with doctors and patients.

Scan

Find the answers to these questions as quickly as you can. Raise your hand to show your instructor when you have finished.

1. Circle at least one word in the reading with each of these prefixes and suffixes. Some words might contain more than one.
    a. **allo–**
    b. **auto–**
    c. **bio–**
    d. **–blast**
    e. **chondro–**
    f. **–clast**
    g. **fibro–**
    h. **graft**
    i. **hema–**
    i. **osteo–**
    j. **–toma**

2. What is the definition of an osteoblast? _____

    _____

3. What process is described in four steps? _____

    _____

4. Who is Dr. Antonios Mikos? _____

    _____

5. Which of these organizational patterns does the reading follow?
    a. general background; current problems; future solutions
    b. current situation; analysis of past mistakes; recommendation for future action
    c. presentation of problem; arguments for one side; arguments for the other side
    d. proposal of new method; advantages; disadvantages; recommendation

Read

Read the excerpt from an online journal. For this reading, do not look up any of the underlined words. You may look up other words if you wish.

Using Plastic to Mend Broken Bones

1 Physicians who treat broken bones are excited by research at Rice University in Houston, Texas involving the use of a biodegradable plastic. Traditionally, a broken bone is set by a doctor and then <u>encased</u> in a cast that keeps the limb immobile. This allows the body to heal itself. But how exactly does that happen? Let's take a look.

2 You might think of a bone as something already dead, possibly because the only bones you've ever seen were outside of the body for some reason, perhaps in a piece of meat on your dinner plate. However, your bones are composed of living cells and in fact, are constantly renewing themselves in a process known as bone remodeling. Three types of cells are mainly responsible for this process: osteoclasts, which break down old bone; osteoblasts, which create new bone tissue, and chondroblasts, which form new cartilage. When a bone breaks, if there are no complications, the body heals itself with this process:

1. Blood from broken blood vessels forms a clot, known as a fracture hematoma, which helps to stabilize the ends of the broken bone and keep them in place.

2. After several days, the fracture hematoma becomes tougher, and fibroblasts, cells that produce collagen, begin strengthening the bone further.

3. Next, chondroblasts begin to create cartilage to join the two pieces of bone, forming a callus that lasts for about three weeks.

4. Osteoblasts now begin to form bone cells, changing the callus into a bone callus, which lasts for 3–4 months, protecting the bone as it finishes healing. Osteoblasts and osteoclasts work together for several more months to replace the bone callus with harder bone and restore the bone to its original shape.

3 To protect the body while a broken bone is mending, doctors typically surround the area with a hard cast. Going about one's daily business with a cast can be <u>awkward</u> and difficult; in addition, the skin under the cast can become itchy or even infected, and muscles under the cast that cannot be used begin to <u>atrophy</u>.

4 Furthermore, in complex breaks, so much bone might be <u>shattered</u> that the body cannot manufacture enough new bone to repair the break. Up to now, the most common way to address this situation has been with an autograft, taking a piece of bone from another part of the patient's body, or an allograft, taking a piece of bone from a <u>deceased</u> person. Both methods have their disadvantages, though; an autograft leaves another part of the person's body weaker, and in the case of an allograft, the dead tissue cannot regrow the way living tissue can.

5 Now, however, Dr. Antonios Mikos, a chemist at Rice University, believes he and his team of researchers may have found an answer to the inconvenience and difficulty of casts, autografts, and allografts: plastic.

6 Doctors can inject a solution containing biodegradable plastic into the fracture site. The plastic helps hold the bony parts together in the way of a clot or calus, though it's stronger. In addition, the plastic solution contains stem cells, taken from bone marrow, that will grow into new bone. As the plastic degrades, proteins are released that attract new blood vessels and cells into the area to nourish the growing bone. When the plastic has biodegraded, what's left is the new bone.

7 The process has several advantages. For one thing, since the solution can be injected, doctors don't need to perform surgery in complex situations. The plastic solution can be adjusted for thicker bones such as leg bones or lighter bones such facial bones. Scientists can also control the rate at which the plastic degrades. It's important that the plastic degrade at the same rate as the new bone grows. If the plastic degrades too quickly, then there isn't enough support for the fractured area. If it doesn't degrade quickly enough, the new bone won't be able to form correctly.

8 Some challenges remain. Different bones need different types of plastic solution, too, so the scientists are still adjusting formulas and developing new formulas. Still, the time might not be far off when we can use plastics not only to set broken bones but also to cope with the <u>degeneration</u> of aging bones in the elderly and to counteract birth defects.

Post-Reading Activities

Main Ideas

Answer these questions about the main ideas of the reading.

1. Check and correct (if necessary) your guesses from the second Predict question (page 77).

2. What is the main idea of the reading?
   a. More doctors are using plastic to treat broken bones than ever before.
   b. Plastic has disadvantages as well as advantages in medical treatments.
   c. Plastic has advantages over traditional healing techniques for treating broken bones.

3. Why is it important for a healing bone to be held in one position?
   a. so that the area doesn't become infected
   b. so that new bone can be grown to join the broken parts
   c. so that doctors can work accurately on the damaged area

4. What are the functions of these cells?

   osteoblasts: _____

   osteoclasts: _____

   chondroblasts: _____

   fibroblasts:_____

Details

Circle the correct word or phrase to complete the sentences.

1. Traditionally, doctors put *a cast / collagen* on a patient's limb while it was healing.

2. A fracture hematoma keeps the broken bone *warm / steady*.

3. It can take about six *weeks / months* for a broken bone to fully heal.

4. Keeping a cast on the body can damage a person's skin and *bones / muscles*.

5. The plastic solution is convenient to apply because it can be *made quickly / injected*.

6. The plastic solution also contains *protein / vitamins*.

7. The plastic solution helps bone regrow *more quickly / less painfully*.

8. Researchers want to develop solutions that *are cheaper to manufacture / can be used for different types of bones*.

 ## Vocabulary

Read the sentences from the reading again. Circle the best synonym for the underlined words. Do not use a dictionary.

1. Traditionally, a broken bone is set by a doctor and then <u>encased in</u> a cast that keeps the limb immobile.
   a. surrounded by; put inside
   b. strengthened with

2. Going about one's daily business with a cast can be <u>awkward</u> and difficult . . .
   a. common; popular
   b. embarrassing; uncomfortable

3. . . . muscles under the cast that cannot be used begin to <u>atrophy</u>.
   a. get larger and stronger
   b. get smaller and weaker

4. Furthermore, in complex breaks, so much bone might be <u>shattered</u> that the body cannot manufacture enough new bone to repair the break.

   a. broken

   b. created

5. . . . an allograft, taking a piece of bone from a <u>deceased</u> person . . . in the case of an allograft, the dead tissue cannot regrow the way living tissue can.

   a. dead

   b. living

6. . . . also to cope with the <u>degeneration</u> of aging bones in the elderly and counteract birth defects.

   a. new growth

   b. loss of function

Talk with a partner. Answer these questions. Then share your ideas with another pair.

7. Think about the affixes you studied on page 76. How can you remember the difference among these words?

   osteoblast, osteoclast, and *chondroblast*

   autograft and *allograft*

8. Look at the words you circled when you did the Scan activity on page 78. Which ones do you think it's important to know how to pronounce? What other new vocabulary from this reading do you think it's important to know how to pronounce?

Reading Skills: Identifying Informed Opinions

Work with a partner. Read these statements. Write F if the statement is a fact, O if the statement is an opinion, or IO if the statement is an informed opinion. Discuss your choices.

1. Physicians who treat broken bones are excited by research at Rice University in Houston, Texas involving the use of a biodegradable plastic. _____

2. However, your bones are composed of living cells and, in fact, are constantly renewing themselves in a process known as bone remodeling. _____

3. Next, chondroblasts begin to create cartilage to join the two pieces of bone, forming a callus that lasts for about three weeks. _____

4. Going about one's daily business with a cast can be awkward and difficult. _____

5. Furthermore, in complex breaks, so much bone might be shattered that the body cannot manufacture enough new bone to repair the break. _____

6. Both methods have their disadvantages, though; an autograft leaves another part of the person's body weaker, and in the case of an allograft, the dead tissue cannot regrow the way living tissue can.
   _____

7. The plastic helps hold the bony parts together in the way of a clot or calus, though it's stronger. _____

8. It's important that the plastic degrade at the same rate as the new bone grows. _____

9. Some challenges remain. _____

10. Still, the time might not be far off when we can use plastics not only to set broken bones but also to cope with the degeneration of aging bones in the elderly and to counteract birth defects. _____

Understanding the Text

Circle the best answer.

1. Why does the reading begin with a description of how broken bones heal without plastic? Circle as many as apply.

    a. Readers probably don't know the process already.

    b. It makes the information detailed enough to publish in an article.

    c. It makes it possible to understand why the new method is advantageous.

    d. It introduces some necessary medical vocabulary.

    e. It is more common for bones to heal this way than with the new plastic solution.

    f. Some new theories have been proposed about the way that bones heal.

2. Why does the reading number the four steps of the healing process?

    a. to show that healing with the plastic solution goes through the same steps

    b. to clearly show the separate stages of healing

    c. to emphasize that the process takes four months

3. What is the writer's attitude towards the plastic solution?

    a. neutral

    b. generally positive

    c. generally negative

4. Why did the writer choose not to include any interviews with patients who have undergone this process?

    a. It hasn't been used on real patients yet.

    b. That kind of information is based on opinions, not facts.

    c. It isn't useful or relevant information.

Extension

Discuss these questions with a partner or a small group, or write a paragraph of response for each.

1. Would you accept being one of the first patients to receive this plastic solution as a treatment? Why or why not?

2. Why might some people object to having plastic injected into their bodies? Should they be allowed to refuse this treatment if a doctor recommends it? Why or why not?

Reading 2: Environmental Studies

Pre-Reading Activities

Identifying Tone: Humor

Recognizing tone can be a lot more difficult in written texts than when you're listening to someone talk. You can't hear a tone of voice the way you can on a telephone, or watch facial expressions or body language the way you can when you're facing someone. You can't hear laughter from an audience the way you can in a lecture or group discussion. Without these cues, it can be tricky sometimes to tell what the writer's mood is or when a writer is serious or making a joke. In the United States in particular, even "serious" writers mix humor into their writing sometimes. This does not mean that their articles do not also contain facts, valid arguments, and important information. However, it is essential that in such an article you be able to distinguish between humor, fact, and opinion. There are several types of humor that can cause difficulty in written texts.

EXAGGERATION

Everything I buy these days is wrapped in three layers of plastic.

The writer doesn't mean that "everything" is wrapped in "three layers" of plastic; rather, the writer is saying that too many purchases are wrapped in plastic, and that also too much plastic is used in many wrappings.

UNDERSTATEMENT

Spending 45 minutes with a knife trying to get the plastic case off a new CD is a little annoying.

Here, the writer is actually more than "a little" annoyed.

SARCASM

I was so pleased to discover that the "wooden" floors and cabinets in my new house were actually made from plastic, because plastic is so much more beautiful.

A sarcastic sentence actually has the opposite meaning of what it seems to say at first. Sarcasm can be difficult to judge in a single sentence. However, if you know that the example sentence here is sarcastic, then you know that the writer is actually saying that he/she does not prefer plastic to wood as a building material.

COMPARISONS and ANALOGIES

Saying that guns cause deaths in the United States is like saying that flies cause garbage.

The invention of plastic was as important to manufacturing as the invention of steel.

Sometimes these can be very effective; sometimes, however, the writer is actually comparing two situations that are so dissimilar that he or she does not really prove the point. The first example, while it might be humorous, is not helpful. Guns and flies are not similar. The second example is more thoughtful. Not everyone will agree, but the writer could explain further with arguments and examples to support the opinion. It's important to ask yourself when considering comparisons whether the two things being compared are actually similar enough for the comparison to be valid.

Vocabulary

Match the word on the left to its definition on the right. You may use a dictionary. Then complete the sentences on page 89 with the correct form of the words.

1. **ban** _____

2. **clog** _____

3. **compressed** _____

4. **contaminated** _____

5. **impose** _____

6. **landfill** _____

7. **leach** _____

8. **overstated** _____

9. **scourge** v

10. **underwhelm** _____

11. **vanishing** _____

12. **volume** _____

a. something that causes widespread, serious harm, such as a disease or war

b. explained or expressed with exaggeration

c. to stop movement; to clutter or block

d. to be dissolved

e. disappearing

f. unclean; impure; poisoned

g. to not impress someone; to be disappointing

h. to forbid or prevent something

i. an amount (of something)

j. reduced the size of something by pressure

k. a site where garbage is deposited and then buried

l. to force (something; usually unpleasant) on (someone)

a. Don't flush anything except toilet paper down a toilet, or you will
_____ the pipes.

b. No one voted for the new law. Instead, it was _____ on
them.

c. The _____ of old computers and cell phones is growing
at an alarming rate.

d. Malaria is the _____ of some nations.

e. The government just _____ the use of that dangerous
chemical with a new law.

f. The cardboard boxes were flattened and then _____ to
fit into a smaller space.

g. Several species of animals are endangered in our area because their
habitats are _____ as they are converted to farmland.

h. If you don't recycle your trash, it will end up in the
_____.

i. Some people worry that particles from plastic containers will
_____ into food if the food is stored inside them for too
long.

j. I paid a lot of money to hear him speak, but I was
_____. I didn't think he did a good job at all.

k. Unfortunately, the river has been _____ by chemical
waste from the nearby factories.

l. I think that report _____ the dangers of using plastic
containers. I think the risk is very, very small.

Predict

Work with a partner. Read the first paragraph of the reading on page 91. Guess what the writer's opinion will be. Then read the conclusion on page 92. Did it express the same opinion as the introduction or a different one? What do you think the middle of the reading will say?

Skim

Skim the reading (pages 91–92) quickly. Then circle your answers to the questions.

1. The reading will be *easy / medium / difficult* for me to understand.

2. The reading is *mainly facts / mainly opinions*.

3. The reading *does / does not* contain information from other sources.

Scan

Find the answers to these questions as quickly as you can. Raise your hand to show your instructor when you have finished.

1. How much money does the City Council want to charge per plastic bag? _____

2. Where are most reusable bags manufactured?_____

3. What city has already banned plastic bags in grocery stores? _____

4. What percentage of waste in landfills is made up of plastic? _____

Read

Read the editorial letter from a newspaper. Underline up to six words to check in a dictionary as you read.

Bagging Plastic?

1 Citizens, our town is under attack again. Worse than cigarettes, worse than potholes, worse even than taxes . . . are plastic bags. This is why the City Council has, in its wisdom, proposed to save us from this scourge by imposing a 15-cent charge on each plastic bag you take from the grocery store.

2 Their reasoning? The manufacture of plastic harms the environment. Plastic bags are expensive to recycle, and often people don't recycle them but merely—gasp!—throw them away; or, worse, litter them about the countryside. Clearly, the harmful effects of plastic bags on the environment cannot be overstated.

3 Or can they?

4 Yes, the lack of biodegradable materials used in the manufacture of plastic bags can cause an excessive buildup of landfills. Yes, they can clog the world's waters and leach toxic chemicals into them, although at an infinitesimally slow rate. But focusing on plastic bags as the primary cause of the world's environmental woes is like focusing on lightning strikes as the leading cause of accidental death. Yes, it's one cause of the problem, but it's a pretty small one in the grand scheme of things.

5 When we look around the globe at all of the problems caused by climate

Plastic does not go away.

change, such as vanishing habitats and the accelerating extinction of animal species, the inconvenience of clearing out plastic bags seems pretty insignificant. Having air that is breathable seems just a bit more important than worrying about air contaminated by the occasional plastic bag blowing past. To the billions of people faced with the prospect of basic drinking water being unavailable, the threat of plastic bags underwhelms.

6 Besides, it's not as if the alternatives to plastic bags are clearly better. Paper bags are not environmentally neutral. There's the necessity of generating the paper in the first place from trees, and the chemicals used in their manufacture can also pose some toxic problems. In fact, it takes four times

A typical plastic shopping bag

as much energy to manufacture a paper bag as a plastic one. Paper is heavier than plastic, too, and thicker; in fact, to transport the same number of paper bags to the store as plastic bags takes seven times as many trucks—and you know how much fuel those large trucks use up.

7 Those re-usable cloth bags that all of the friends of the earth are so proud to carry aren't necessarily the best environmental choice either. Most of those bags are manufactured in China—and then shipped here to the US, using far more fossil fuels than plastic bags made here at home.

8 Some cities, such as San Francisco, have already banned plastic bags at the grocery stores. So this means that people who would normally re-use their grocery bags to line their trash cans at home or carry things around must now actually purchase plastic bags (which I suppose they carry home in their made-from-trees paper bags or their shipped-from-China reusable bags). How is this a better environmental choice?

9 According to the Environmental Literacy Council's website, plastics (not just bags) account for 14 to 28 percent of the volume of trash in general. However, because much of it can be compressed, plastic makes up only 9 to 12 percent of the volume of waste in landfills. And when you think of what a small portion of all plastic waste must come from those light bags, the "problem" seems even more insignificant.

10 The whole argument reminds me of automakers who are spending thousands, if not millions, of dollars to develop an SUV that gets an additional two miles to the gallon. The problem with cars isn't whether a vehicle gets 24 miles to the gallon or 26. The problem is that cities are designed in such a way that Americans are overly dependent on driving personal vehicles. The answer is denser cities with good public transportation, not a slightly improved personal automobile.

11 Similarly, the "answer" at the store is not what bag you take your purchases home in. The answer is what and how much you buy in the first place. If people only bought what they needed, not a new shirt every week or a new cell phone every three months or a lot of useless decorations that they didn't need at all, then it wouldn't matter what kind of bags they used.

12 I'm not saying that it's a bad idea to care for the environment. As I've shown, though, with this law, we'd be forcing shoppers to make environmentally worse choices. But a more crucial point is that by spending time and money on this silliest of issues, plastic bags, we're not paying attention to more important issues. Please. Vote against the 15-cent increase. And let's get serious about addressing environmental problems.

—Paul Martin

Post-Reading Activities

Main Ideas

Circle the answer that best expresses the main ideas of the reading.

1. What is the main purpose of this letter?

    a. to get people to stop using plastic bags

    b. to convince people to vote against something

    c. to argue that plastic bags are better than other kinds of bags

2. What arguments does the writer make? Circle all that apply.

    a. The 15-cent charge is too high for plastic bags.

    b. Plastic bags are cheaper for stores than other bags.

    c. Plastic bags are not a very significant environmental problem.

    d. Plastic bags are not biodegradable.

    e. Making paper bags is worse for the environment than making plastic bags.

    f. Most people think plastic bags are more useful than paper bags.

    g. If people think about plastic bags, they'll ignore more important problems.

    h. Some people, if they can't reuse plastic bags from the grocery store, will buy plastic bags.

    i. Plastic bags are not a significant portion of the garbage in landfills.

    j. The government shouldn't tell people what to buy and what not to buy.

    k. It would be better to use different materials instead of plastic to manufacture most products.

Details

Match the numbers with the corresponding information from the reading.

1. **4** _____

2. **7** _____

3. **9 to 12** _____

4. **14 to 28** _____

5. **15** _____

6. **24 to 26** _____

a. amount of money, in cents, that the City Council wishes to charge shoppers per plastic bag

b. how many more times as much energy it takes to make a paper bag as it does to make a plastic one

c. miles per gallon for SUVs that the writer mentions

d. how many more trucks it takes to transport paper bags as it does to transport plastic bags

e. percentage of trash in a landfill that is plastic

f. percentage of trash in general that is plastic

Vocabulary

Write answers to the questions. Then discuss them with a partner.

1. Did you underline any words to look up? If so, look them up now. Write the words and their definitions.

   a. _____

   b. _____

   c. _____

   d. _____

   e. _____

   f. _____

2. Were the words you chose to look up important to understand the reading? Do you wish you had chosen any different words?

   _____

   _____

3. Read the letter again. Are there other words you don't know? Look up any further words if you think they are important.

   _____

   _____

Reading Skills: Identifying Tone: Humor

Part 1

Read the sentences. Underline the words or phrases that exaggerate. Double-underline the words or phrases that understate.

1. Citizens, our town is under attack again.

2. This is why the City Council has, in its wisdom, proposed to save us from this scourge by imposing a 15-cent charge on each plastic bag you take from the grocery store.

3. Clearly, the harmful effects of plastic bags on the environment cannot be overstated.

4. When we look around the globe at all of the problems caused by climate change, such as vanishing habitats and the accelerating extinction of animal species, the inconvenience of clearing out plastic bags seems pretty insignificant.

5. Having air that is breathable seems just a bit more important than worrying about air contaminated by the occasional plastic bag blowing past.

6. To the billions of people faced with the prospect of basic drinking water being unavailable, the threat of plastic bags underwhelms.

7. Those re-usable cloth bags that all of the friends of the earth are so proud to carry aren't necessarily the best environmental choice either.

8. If people only bought what they needed, not a new shirt every week or a new cell phone every three months or a lot of useless decorations that they didn't need at all, then it wouldn't matter what kind of bags they used.

9. But a more crucial point is that by spending time and money on this silliest of issues, plastic bags, we're not paying attention to more important issues.

Part 2

Work with a partner. Evaluate these analogies. Do you think these analogies are helpful? Or are they misleading?

1. But focusing on plastic bags as the primary cause of the world's environmental woes is like focusing on lightning strikes as the leading cause of accidental death.

   _____

   _____

2. The whole argument reminds me of automakers who are spending thousands, if not millions, of dollars to develop an SUV that gets an additional two miles to the gallon.

   _____

   _____

Understanding the Text

Work with a partner. Complete the exercises.

1. Write F if the statement is a fact, O if the statement is an opinion, or IO if the statement is an informed opinion.

   a. The manufacture of plastic harms the environment. _____

   b. Yes, the lack of biodegradable materials used in the manufacture of plastic bags can cause an excessive buildup of landfills. _____

   c. Paper bags are not environmentally neutral. _____

   d. In fact, it takes four times as much energy to manufacture a paper bag as a plastic one. _____

   e. Most of those bags are manufactured in China. _____

   f. According to the Environmental Literacy Council's website, plastics (not just bags) account for 14 to 28 percent of the volume of trash in general. _____

   g. The problem is that cities are designed in such a way that Americans are overly dependent on driving personal vehicles. _____

   h. As I've shown, though, with this law, we'd be forcing shoppers to make environmentally worse choices. _____

2. Discuss the author's tone. How would you describe it? Did his tone make the letter seem more believable, less believable, or not have an effect?

3. How many of the author's arguments did you find believable?

4. Were you persuaded to agree with the author's main purpose? Why or why not?

5. If you were asked to write a paper for an environmental studies class about the impact of plastic bags on the environment, which information or arguments in the letter would be useful for you? Which would not be useful for you?

6. *To bag something* is an informal way of saying "to get rid of something," "to throw something away," or "to stop using something." Work with a partner. What is the joke in the reading's title, "Bagging Plastic"? Why does the writer choose a humorous title? Do you think it is effective?

Extension

Discuss these questions with a small group, or write a paragraph of response for each.

1. Do you agree that the issue of plastic bags is not an important one? Why or why not? Whether the issue is significant or not, is it still one that people should think about?

2. Is what kind of bags stores use an issue for stores to decide, or the government, or shoppers, or someone else? Support your answer.

3. Make a quick list of some small things that people can do to help the environment. Then make a quick list of some larger issues that local governments should address. Finally, make a quick list of some larger issues that national governments should address. Share your lists with the class.

Wolves

Discuss

Discuss these questions with a small group.

1. What do you already know about wolves? What are some of your impressions of wolves?

2. In what kind of habitats do wolves live? What do they eat?

3. What are some problems that might arise if wolves lived close to areas where people live? Should wolves be kept away from people?

Reading 1: Zoology

Pre-Reading Activities

Dictionary Skills 2: Recognizing the Right Definition

Words in English, as in other languages, often have more than one meaning. Sometimes the meanings are related, but other times they are completely different. When you check a new word in a dictionary, therefore, it's very important to make sure that you find the definition that fits your word in its specific context.

The first thing to check is the part of speech. Is your unknown word being used as a noun, verb, adjective, or adverb? Sometimes you can tell from the suffix of the word. Another way to determine the part of speech is from the context of the sentence.

For example, if you don't know the meaning of the word *rock*, and you check a dictionary, you will find it listed as a verb, meaning "to move back and forth," and also as a noun, meaning "a large stone." The meanings are entirely different. However, if you look at the context, you can often determine the part of speech.

The wolf climbed onto a large **rock** *to look over the valley.*

You can tell that *rock* is being used as a noun.

Next, you need to check the meaning of the rest of the sentence, and even the sentences before and after. They might not tell you exactly what the unknown word means, but you will know when you find the right "fit."

The social unit of wolves is the **pack***. They travel, hunt, and live in this group.*

In the sentence, you can tell that the word *pack* is a noun. You would not, therefore, be tempted to select the dictionary definition of pack as *the action of putting clothes and belongings into a suitcase*. A *pack*, the noun, can mean *a backpack*, or *a group of animals*, or even *a large amount of something*, like *a pack of trouble*. But if you are thinking about a social unit of wolves, then only the definition of *a group of animals* makes any sense.

Practice Recognizing the Right Definition

Read the sentences. Write the part of speech of the underlined word. Then copy a dictionary definition for that word. For this exercise, use an English-English dictionary, although you may also use a native language dictionary to double-check the meaning if necessary.

1. Wolf communication is a fascinating field of study. Many field biologists have been studying <u>lupine</u> packs for years to gather information in this area.

   Part of speech: _____

   Definition: _____

2. When a wolf is angry, the fur on the back of its neck <u>bristles</u> and its ears flatten.

   Part of speech: _____

   Definition: _____

3. It's important for a young wolf to show its <u>submission</u> to an older, more powerful male.

   Part of speech: _____

   Definition: _____

4. The leader of the pack, the alpha male, is the most <u>dominant</u> member.

   Part of speech: _____

   Definition: _____

5. A wolf might "speak" by giving a <u>bark</u>, a howl, or a growl to another member of the pack.

   Part of speech: _____

   Definition: _____

6. If you see a wolf <u>narrow</u> its eyes, it is probably feeling aggressive or threatened.

   Part of speech: _____

   Definition: _____

7. A wolf will crouch down low and tense its leg muscles as it gets ready to <u>spring</u>.

   Part of speech: _____

   Definition: _____

Predict

Work with a partner. The reading on pages 103–5 is about communication among wolves. How do you think wolves communicate? What do you think they communicate about?

Skim

Skim the reading quickly. Then circle your answers to the questions.

1. The reading will be *easy / medium / difficult* for me to understand.

2. Wolves communicate in *three / four / five* main ways.

3. There are *two / three / four* main examples of body language.

Scan

Find the answers to these questions as quickly as you can. Raise your hand to show your instructor when you have finished.

1. What animal is mentioned in addition to the wolf? _____

2. What does a "smiling" face on a wolf indicate? _____

3. What does a wagging tail indicate? _____

4. What is 100 times stronger in a wolf than in a human? _____

5. What are five sounds that a wolf makes? _____

Read

Read the excerpt from a textbook. Do not look up any of the underlined words. You will have a chance to look them up later. You may look up any other words if you wish.

Communication among Wolves

1 A central purpose of a great deal of wolf communication within the pack is to establish position, especially in terms of dominance and submission. To wolves, it is very important to know which animal is in charge. Communication with wolves outside the pack is more territorial; that is, packs <u>mark</u> their territories and warn away strangers or intruders. Wolves communicate mainly through body language, scent, and sound.

Body language

2 Body posture and movements of ears, tail, etc., signal lupine affection, fear, aggression, happiness, and other feelings, as well as <u>position</u> within the pack.

Wolves in a pack

3 **Posture.** A dominant wolf stands erect, with its head up. A submissive wolf, on the other hand, will crouch down, bow its head, or lower its shoulders. A submissive wolf might paw at the ground of a more dominant wolf, or even bite the dominant wolf lightly under the chin. You may see a fully submissive wolf lie on its back at the feet of the dominant wolf, exposing its belly. When threatened, a wolf can actually enlarge its apparent body size by raising its hackles and bristling its fur; this may cause a smaller opponent to back away. Dominant wolves walk proudly, taking larger steps than more submissive wolves; dominant wolves might actually

bump into more subordinate wolves while they are walking as a display of their power.

Is this wolf smiling?

4 Face. Dog owners will tell you that their dog's face can show happiness as clearly as a human's. Similarly, a wolf with an open mouth and tongue hanging out can look as if it is "smiling," and this does indeed indicate happiness or playfulness. A wolf who feels anxious or scared will keep its mouth shut with the lips pulled back, and will lower its ears. Reacting to a threat, a wolf will wrinkle its nose, narrow its eyes, open its mouth to bare its teeth, and raise its ears. A wolf who is frightened will flatten the ears against its head. Ears lightly pulled back can show suspicion. Direct eye contact is another way in which a wolf can dominate another wolf or even an animal from another species. Sometimes an intense stare from a wolf is all that is necessary to turn away a more <u>subordinate</u> pack member.

5 Tail. As with dogs, a wagging tail is a sign of happiness or playfulness. A tall, erect tail shows dominance; conversely, a submissive wolf will lower its tail or tuck the tail just between its hind legs. The tail tucked more fully under the body, together with an arched back, shows that the wolf is afraid. A tail in a <u>roughly</u> horizontal position, held stiffly, indicates a hunting wolf. A relaxed, dropped tail shows a correspondingly relaxed animal.

Scent

6 Wolves have a keen sense of smell, which is about 100 times as strong as a human's. They can smell prey at a distance of up to three kilometers (1.75 miles). Wolves mark their territory by urinating on trees, rocks, and such. Generally, the dominant wolves of the pack, in

particular the alpha male, do most of this marking. A wolf from another pack can tell from the scent that the territory is occupied. Wolves can also mark food <u>caches</u> as empty in a similar fashion. That way, a pack member who comes upon the cache will not waste its time digging there for buried food.

Sound

7 Like dogs, wolves bark and growl; however, their distinctive sound is the howl. Packs of wolves howl most often at twilight and at night, since wolves are most active then. A wolf's howl can act as a signal to call other wolves in its pack to indicate location; this is especially useful as packs move through thickly forested areas where visibility is low. Wolves also howl to warn away members of other packs. Some researchers believe that wolves also howl before a hunt to increase their energy levels. A short bark can be used to scare away enemies, as can a <u>low</u> growl. Growling also is used to <u>assert</u> dominance within the pack. Whining and whimpering can accompany submissive body language to a dominant wolf.

A wolf howls

Post-Reading Activities

Main Ideas and Details

Match the word on the left with its definition on the right.

1. baring _____   a. pulling up or hiding something

2. biting _____   b. bending legs to be lower

3. bristling _____   c. uncovering

4. crouching _____   d. grabbing something with teeth

5. erect _____   e. touching or scraping with a leg

6. direct _____   f. straight or tall

7. pawing _____   g. rising to stand straight (used for hair or fur)

8. tucking _____   h. straight and without interruption

For each description, write if the wolf's message is dominant or submissive.

1. making direct eye contact   _____

2. bristling its fur along its back   _____

3. baring its teeth   _____

4. pawing at the ground   _____

5. crouching down around others   _____

6. tucking its tail between its legs   _____

7. holding its tail erect   _____

8. biting another wolf's chin   _____

Reading Skills: Dictionary Skills: Recognizing the Right Definition

Part 1

Read the sentences from the reading again. Find the correct definition for the underlined words in an English-English dictionary, and write it on the lines. Then share your definitions with a partner.

1. . . . packs <u>mark</u> their territories and warn away strangers or intruders.

   _____

2. Body posture and movements of ears, tail, etc., signal . . . <u>position</u> within the pack.

   _____

3. Sometimes an intense stare from a wolf is all that is necessary to turn away a more <u>subordinate</u> pack member.

   _____

4. A tail in a <u>roughly</u> horizontal position, held stiffly, indicates a hunting wolf.

   _____

5. Wolves can also mark food <u>caches</u> as empty in a similar fashion.

   _____

6. A short bark can be used to scare away enemies, as can a <u>low</u> growl.

   _____

7. Growling also is used to <u>assert</u> dominance within the pack.

   _____

Part 2

Work with a partner. Discuss how you could remember the difference between these pairs of words.

1. dominant / submissive _____

2. howl / growl _____

_____

Understanding the Text

Circle the best answer for this reading. Then discuss the questions with a partner or small group.

1. Which type of communication do you think is the most important? Why?

   a. body language

   b. scent

   c. sound

2. Which type of body language do you think is the most important? Why?

   a. posture

   b. face

   c. tail

3. Check (✓) the methods of support the text uses to explain communication in a wolf pack.

   _____ anecdotes

   _____ charts and graphs

   _____ comparisons with other animals

   _____ descriptions

   _____ direct quotes from experts

   _____ examples

   _____ logical explanations

   _____ photographs

   _____ results of scientific studies

Extension

Discuss these questions with a partner or small group, or write a paragraph of response to each.

1. Imagine you are alone in the woods and are faced by an angry wolf. What body language could you use to show submission and thus avoid an attack?

2. Do you consider lupine communication to be "language"? Why or why not?

Reading 2: Urban Planning
Pre-Reading Activities

Annotating as You Read

If you are reading large amounts of material and concentrating mostly on main ideas and general concepts, it's useful to write notes in the margins that summarize the main ideas of each paragraph. (If you are using a library book, write these notes on sticky notes.) These notes are called annotations. If paragraphs contain important specific information, such as dates, highlight these with a colored marker.

The challenge in summarizing a paragraph is often figuring out which information is the most important. Sometimes this is contained in the topic sentence, which may be the first sentence or the last one. This is especially common in textbooks. However, the topic sentence is not always first, and not every paragraph has one.

The process of judging which information is the most important, putting it in your own words, and then writing it will help you enormously in both understanding your reading and in remembering the information.

Practice Annotating

Read the first paragraph, and decide which annotation would be best. Discuss your choice with a partner. Then write an annotation for the second paragraph.

1. In 1995, 14 wolves were reintroduced into Yellowstone Park. These wolves came from several different packs. For one thing, it's difficult to capture an entire wild wolf pack—alive, that is. Furthermore, wolves from different packs carried a greater variety of genes, ensuring that their offspring would be healthier (they couldn't mate with wolves from other packs, after all, since there were no other packs). Biologists selected a dominant male and a dominant female wolf and placed them in a holding pen with a group of submissive wolves, and within 24 hours, the wolves had figured out the new pack social order.

    a. Only 14 wolves were chosen for the new pack in Yellowstone in 1995.

    b. 1995: Yellowstone's first new pack: made up of wolves from different packs because (1) only way possible and (2) made healthier new pack.

    c. Biologists discovered that wolves can form a new pack in 24 hours if the right wolves are chosen.

2. An average wolf pack in the wild consists of six to eight members, typically an alpha male, an alpha female, and their offspring. How large the pack is depends on the amount of prey available within the pack's territory and how many other wolves live in the same area. If there isn't much food and there are competing wolves in the area, then female wolves might not give birth in a given season. However, if the opposite is true, the females can give birth to many pups.

    _____

    _____

    _____

    _____

    _____

Vocabulary

Read the sentences. Write the part of speech above the underlined word: N for noun, V for verb, or Adj. for adjective. Then check the meaning of the underlined words in a dictionary.

1. That wolf was raised in <u>captivity</u>. It has been held <u>captive</u> for two years now.

2. Although it can be difficult to <u>breed</u> some species of wild animals, such <u>breeding</u> programs are essential for their survival.

3. Raising <u>livestock</u> is challenging because of weather and natural predators.

4. <u>Endangered</u> <u>species</u> need legal protection to keep them from becoming <u>extinct</u>.

5. Special <u>recovery</u> programs have helped the gray wolf in the United States. However, not all species have <u>recovered</u> equally well.

6. The <u>habitat</u> of the wolf disappears as cities and farms continue to spread.

Predict

Work with a partner. The reading on pages 113–15 is about bringing a subspecies of wolf back into an area in the United States from which it had disappeared. Discuss these questions.

1. Why do you think the wolves disappeared?

2. Why are people interested in bringing them back?

3. What kind of people might not want the wolves to come back?

4. What do you think are some challenges the new wolves faced?

5. Do you think the program was successful?

Skim

Skim the reading quickly. Then answer the questions.

1. The reading will be *easy / medium / difficult* for me to understand.

2. The reading contains *mostly facts / mostly opinions / a mix of facts and opinions.*

3. The reading contains (check all that apply):
   ___ graphs
   ___ dates
   ___ quotations
   ___ references to other sources

Scan

Find the answers to these questions as quickly as you can. Raise your hand to show your instructor when you have finished.

1. What type of wolf is mainly discussed in the article? _____

2. In what year did the wolf's luck change? _____

3. When was the Mexican Gray Wolf Recovery Plan passed? _____

4. How many wolves were initially released into the wild? _____

5. Where were they released? _____

6. How many wolves were living in the wild in 2008? _____

7. How many cattle were killed by wolves since their reintroduction? ___

8. What or who are the WildEarth Guardians, The Rewilding Institute, and the Center for Biological Diversity? _____
   _____

Read

Read the article from a website. Underline up to six words you would like to look up in a dictionary later. Annotate each paragraph as you read.

Reintroduction of the Mexican Gray Wolf: Successes and Challenges

<u>Annotations</u>

1   The Mexican gray wolf (canis lupis baileyi) used to roam freely over the southwestern portion of the United States, in the area now divided up as Texas, New Mexico, Arizona, and Mexico. However, with the settling of the area by humans in the early 1900s, wolves were either hunted for food, killed to protect livestock, or simply lost their habitat to houses and farmland. By 1970, the wolves were almost entirely eliminated from the area as a result of efforts by not only private citizens but also state and federal organizations.

2   The wolf's luck changed in 1976, the year it was listed as a subspecies of the gray wolf, already protected under the 1973 Endangered Species Act. Now the U.S. Fish and Wildlife Service had a new mission: not only to protect the wolf, but to actually bring it back from the brink of extinction. At that time, there were only a few scattered reports of the Mexican gray wolf in the wild, mostly from Mexico.

3   From 1977 to 1982, several measures were taken in the recovery of the Mexican gray wolf. Mexico and the U.S. worked together on a captive breeding program with wolves trapped in Mexico; this was essential to build up the number of wolves in existence and save the species from total extinction. A wolf recovery team was established in the U.S. in 1979 to help with

A gray wolf in a tree in a nature preserve

planning. The plan recommended releasing at least 100 captive Mexican gray wolves into the mountains in Mexico. Finally, in 1982, the Mexican Gray Wolf Recovery Plan was passed.

Annotations

4   During this time, attention was focused nationally on the status of the gray wolf, which had roamed over most of the United States at one point, but had been hunted to near extinction during the early to mid 1900s. In 1978, the Service listed the entire gray wolf species as endangered (except in Minnesota where it was listed as threatened). For most other subspecies of the gray wolf, animals could be relocated from Canada; in fact, only the Mexican gray wolf was so rare that its population had to be built up from the captive breeding program.

5   On March 29, 1998, 11 wolves from the breeding program were released into the Gila National Forest in New Mexico, near the Arizona border. The hope was for there to be 100 wolves in the wild and at least 18 breeding pairs by 2006.

6   However, the wolves had a rough time. The first wolf released was shot and killed (illegally). More later suffered the same fate; the first pup born in the wild died after its mother was shot. More adult wolves died than had been expected and fewer new pups lived. Some strayed out of their official areas (wolves can't read maps) and had to be relocated; not all survived their relocation. A controversial law states that any wolf that has been involved in three or more livestock kills per year must be removed or destroyed; in 2007, for example, 22 cows and calves in the area were killed by wolves. Ironically, therefore, the Service itself contributed to the deaths of 25 of the wolves either through killing them outright or because the wolves died while being held captive or being moved.

7   By the end of 2008, a survey showed only 52 wolves spread out over New Mexico and Arizona.

8   The largest opposition to the Mexican wolf currently comes from livestock ranchers, who strongly objected to the return of the wolves and are not happy about further efforts to help them. According to the executive director of the New Mexico Cattle Growers' Association, Caren Cowan, about 1,500 cattle were killed by wolves in the 11 years after reintroduction. "Some people say in 11 years that's not a lot of cows, but multiply that by $1,000 per animal, and that's a lot," she said. The group Defenders of Wildlife, which points out that cattle make up only four percent of the

wolves' diet, pays livestock owners as much as $3,000 per lost animal in an effort to reduce their opposition to the wolves.

9   Three wildlife organizations, WildEarth Guardians, The Rewilding Institute, and the Center for Biological Diversity, claim that a greater effort and more legal protection is needed to save the Mexican gray wolf. They are arguing to have it listed as a distinct population, separate from the gray wolf, so that it can receive increased attention. They point out that the Mexican wolf's habitat is different from that of the gray wolf, and that it roams 700 miles away from the gray wolf's territory. The groups hope that separate, protected habitat can be set aside for the Mexican gray wolf to keep it away from livestock and populated areas. In areas such as Yellowstone Park, where gray wolves have been reintroduced, recovery has been successful in a large part because no conflict exists with livestock ranchers.

Post-Reading Activities

Main Ideas

Circle the answer that best expresses the main ideas of the reading.

1. Wolves used to *not live / be common* in the U.S.

2. The U.S. and Mexico worked together to *stop wolf hunting / put wolves back in the wild*.

3. The relocated wolves *struggled at first / had an easy time*.

4. Ranchers don't like the wolf recovery play because *it is taking their land / wolves are killing their animals*.

5. The Mexican gray wolf *is still endangered / has a healthy population* now.

Details

Write the date or time period on the lines after the events. Then number them in chronological order on the lines before the events.

___ 22 cows and calves killed by Mexican wolves _____

___ captive breeding program established and other measures taken to help the Mexican gray wolf _____

___ entire gray wolf species listed as endangered _____

___ first Mexican wolves reintroduced into New Mexico _____

___ Mexican gray wolves included in the Endangered Species Act _____

___ passage of the Mexican Gray Wolf Recovery Plan _____

___ only 52 Mexican wolves found in the wild in New Mexico and Arizona _____

___ passage of the Endangered Species Act _____

___ wolves were hunted nearly to extinction in the U.S. _____

Reading Skills: Annotating as You Read

Work in a small group. Share your annotations for each paragraph. Did you each choose to record the same information? List any different choices, and discuss them.

_____

_____

_____

_____

Vocabulary

Write answers to the questions. Then discuss them with a partner.

1. Did you underline any words to look up? If so, write the words and their definitions below.

   a. _____

   b. _____

   c. _____

   d. _____

   e. _____

   f. _____

2. Were the words you chose to look up important to understand the reading? Do you wish you had chosen different words?

3. Read the article again. Are there other words you don't know? Look up any further words if you think they are important.

4. How can you use word parts to remember the meanings of these words?

   a. subspecies _____

   b. extinction _____

   c. recovery _____

   d. relocation _____

   e. controversial _____

   f. reintroduce _____

Understanding the Text

Circle the best answer. Then discuss the questions with a partner or small group.

1. Why does the reading begin with such a long discussion of the history of the Mexican gray wolf?
   a. Most readers won't know what a Mexican gray wolf is.
   b. The wolf's problems today can be traced back to mistakes in earlier laws.
   c. It's important to understand why the wolf disappeared and how hard it is to bring it back.

2. How is the text organized overall?
   a. chronologically
   b. pro-wolf arguments, then anti-wolf arguments
   c. what the United States has done for the wolf, then what Mexico has done

3. What is the tone at the end of the reading?
   a. pessimistic
   b. neutral
   c. cautiously optimistic

Extension

Discuss these questions with a partner or a small group, or write a paragraph of response for each.

1. Is it important to prevent extinction of an animal species? Why or why not?

2. Who has more right to be on an area of land in New Mexico: the livestock or the wolves? Do you think both can exist there at the same time?

3. If wolves come further into areas where people live and begin killing dogs, cats, and other pets, what (if anything) should be done?

4. Do you think it's possible or desirable to introduce large predators such as tigers back into areas where humans now also live?

Rice

Discuss

Discuss these questions with a small group.

1. How often do you eat rice? In what ways is it prepared?

2. What do you know about how rice is grown?

3. What countries in the world do you think consume the most rice? What do non-rice eating countries consume instead?

4. Guess which of the countries in the box are the 12 largest consumers of rice per capita (six countries are not used). Then rank them in order from 1 to 12 (use pencil!). (Check your answers on page 144).

Australia	India	Russia
Bangladesh	Indonesia	South Korea
Burma	Japan	Taiwan
Canada	Mexico	Thailand
China	North Korea	United States
France	Philippines	Vietnam

Reading 1: Biology

Pre-Reading Activities

Identifying Major and Minor Points

There is no one answer to what the difference between a major and a minor point is; it depends on your purpose for reading. A business major might be most interested in amounts of money; a history major in dates; an art major in names of artists; a social scientist in broader concepts. Often, though, details such as numbers and dates are used to emphasize major points. They help you understand how large or small, how important or insignificant, something is. Whether you need to remember the specific figures depends on your purpose for studying that particular material. In every case, though, even if you need to memorize the specific details, you will need to understand the main ideas.

As you read, ask yourself (as you did when annotating the reading about the wolf relocation program on pages 113–15), what the most important point of the paragraph is. Ask yourself after every few paragraphs, what are the most important ideas? And again, after you have finished the reading, ask yourself, what is the most important idea? What overall message or messages is the writer communicating?

Once you have determined the main ideas, think of your reasons for reading. What are you expected to learn? Will you be tested on details or broader concepts? Will you need specific information to support arguments you give in class or write in a research paper? Then go back and reread, paying attention to the specific information that you need.

Vocabulary

Work with a partner. Do you know what these words and expressions mean? Use a dictionary if necessary and write a definition. Then read the sentences and circle the correct answer.

drought   severity

heat wave   strain (n., as in *strain of rice*)

inhibit   submerge

monsoon   tolerant

(rice) paddy   vulnerable

photosynthesis   withstand

resistant

1. The plants died after being *inhibited / submerged* under water.

2. Farmers appreciate varieties of crops that are *vulnerable / resistant* to disease.

3. The strong rains of the *monsoon / paddy* caused flooding in several villages.

4. From time to time, researches develop *new strains / heat waves* of plants in their laboratories.

5. Very few plants can *inhibit / withstand* both very high temperatures and very low temperatures.

6. Unfortunately the government underestimated the *severity / photosynthesis* of the problem.

7. Poor growing conditions can *resist / inhibit* a crop's ability to produce well.

8. Farmers struggled to bring more water to their fields during the *drought / severity*.

Predict

Work with a partner. Look at the title of the reading on page 123, and think about the vocabulary. What do you think the reading will be about?

Skim

Skim the reading (pages 123–24) quickly. Then circle your answers to the questions.

1. The reading will be *easy / medium / difficult* for me to understand.

2. The main problem for rice is *too much / too little* water.

3. Researchers *have found / hope to find* a new strain of rice.

4. The article contains *some / no* statistics.

Scan

Find the answers to these questions as quickly as you can. Raise your hand to show your instructor when you have finished.

1. What are three of the countries mentioned in the reading?

    _____

2. What is the name of the gene that researchers discovered?

    _____

3. Where does Dr. Pamela Ronald work?

    _____

4. How much of the world's rice is eaten in Asia?

    _____

5. What is one problem for rice farmers caused by global warming?

    _____

Read

Read the excerpt from an online news article. Underline up to five words to check in a dictionary later. Annotate each paragraph as you read.

Waterproof Rice

1 Most people, if you ask them to envision a rice paddy, will picture a flooded field, with the rice plants growing up out of the water. However, what many don't realize is that while rice is the only cereal crop that can withstand submergence at all, rice plants will drown if they remain submerged past three or four days. When a rice plant is covered with water, its oxygen and carbon dioxide supplies are reduced, and photosynthesis and respiration are restricted. Without the air and sunlight they need to function, growth is inhibited and the plants eventually die.

2 This is particularly significant because about one fourth of the world's rice is grown in low-lying areas, such as those found in India, Bangladesh, Laos, Indonesia, and the Philippines, that are vulnerable to seasonal flooding and monsoons. Global warming has only worsened the unpredictability as well as the severity of the flooding.

3 However, researchers at the University of California–Davis and the International Rice Research Institute (IRRI) in the Philippines have succeeded in developing a flood-tolerant rice plant that can

A rice field submerged in water.

live under water for about 14 days, or more than three times as long as rice plants can normally withstand being under water. The plants produce as much rice as regular rice varieties and the nutritional quality is good too. The scientists identified a single gene, called Sub1A-1, that makes rice plants more resistant to flooding. One of the team members, Dr. Pamela Ronald, explains, "Our research team anticipates that these newly developed rice varieties will help ensure a more dependable food supply for poor farmers and their families."

4 The biologists tested the rice plants in fields in the target countries themselves. The rice plants performed as well there as they did

Annotations

in test sites, so the researchers put the rice into the hands of the farmers. Many of the farmers cannot read or write, but they "speak rice." Researchers hope that those who struggle with the problems of flooding will embrace the new variety once they see the results for themselves.

5 Rice is essential for the health, if not the very survival, of millions of people—make that about three billion people in Asia. Approximately 90 percent of all the rice in the world is consumed in Asia, especially China, India, and Vietnam. Additionally, those countries that eat the most rice also produce the most rice. In fact, according to the Cambridge World History of Food, more than 95% of the world's rice is eaten by the countries that produce it, rather than sold to the world market. Currently, flooding in the two rice-growing countries of Bangladesh and India reduces the amount of rice produced by up to four million tons. That's enough rice to feed 30 million people. According to Ronald's Web site (http://indica. ucdavis.edu/research/research-project-overviews/submergence _tolerance/), more than 22 million hectares of rice paddies are prone to flooding from seasonal rains. This area is home to 140 million farmers, half of whom live on less than $1 a day.

6 Even as efforts are underway to solve the problems of rice and too much water, scientists are also working on the problems of rice and too little water. As global warming increasingly changes weather patterns, not only flooding but heat waves and droughts are becoming more severe and more common. As sea levels rise, low-lying coastal areas face the threat of salty sea water spilling into the freshwater rice paddies. So scientists are also working to develop strains of rice resistant to high temperatures, drought, and salt water. The only question is whether the development and adoption of new varieties of rice can keep ahead of the pressing need for them.

---

* The initiative is being led by the International Rice Research Institute through grants from the Bill & Melinda Gates Foundation and Japan's Ministry of Foreign Affairs.

** Funding for the research that led to the isolation of the Sub1−A gene came from U.S. Department of Agriculture grants. The breeding work was funded by the German Federal Ministry for Economic Cooperation and Development and the USDA.

Post-Reading Activities

Main Ideas

Work with a small group. Share your annotations for each paragraph. You don't need to agree on your answers, but be able to explain your ideas if there are any differences.

1. Did you each choose to record the same information?

2. Which annotations best capture the main ideas?

Details

Imagine you are taking biology class. Are the ideas listed main ideas or details? Write MI if the statement is a main idea. Write D if the statement is a detail.

1. Most rice plants die if they are submerged in water for more than four days. _____

2. One-fourth of the rice in the world is grown in areas that experience flooding. _____

3. The new strain of waterproof rice can live underwater for up to 14 days. _____

4. The gene responsible for the rice's ability to stay submerged longer is called Sub1A–1. _____

5. The researchers who developed the new strain of rice work at the University of California–Davis and IRRI. _____

6. Many of the farmers who should be interested in this new type of rice are not educated. _____

7. About three billion people in Asia depend on rice to survive. _____

8. More than 95% of the world's rice is eaten in the countries that produce it. _____

9. Many of the farmers affected by flooding live on less than $1 a day. _____

10. Rice crops are also threatened by droughts and the invasion of sea water. _____

Reading Skills: Identifying Major and Minor Points

Write answers to the questions. Then discuss them with with a partner.

1. Of the ideas you labeled as details, which would be important to remember? Why?

   _____

   _____

   _____

   _____

2. How would your answers in the Details activity change if you were taking a class in world affairs instead of biology?

   _____

   _____

   _____

   _____

Vocabulary

Write answers to the questions. Then discuss them with a partner.

1. Did you underline any words to look up? If so, look them up now. Write the words and their definitions.

   a. _____

   b. _____

   c. _____

   d. _____

   e. _____

2. Were the words you chose to look up important to understanding the reading? Do you wish you had chosen any different words?

_____

_____

_____

_____

3. Read the article again. Are there other words you don't know? Look up any further words if you think they are important.

_____

_____

_____

_____

4. Would it be important to know the pronunciation of these words or names? Why or why not?

a. submergence _____

b. photosynthesis _____

c. Bangladesh _____

d. vulnerable _____

e. Dr. Pamela Ronald _____

f. Cambridge World History of Food _____

g. hectares _____

h. drought _____

Understanding the Text

Circle the best answer. Then discuss the questions with a partner or small group.

1. Why doesn't the reading explain in more detail how global warming is affecting rice crops?

   a. It assumes that people already know.

   b. It is too scientific for most readers to understand.

   c. It isn't proven, and might not be true.

2. For whom is this article primarily written?

   a. people in Asia

   b. farmers

   c. a general audience

3. Why does the end of the article list the organizations that funded the research?

   a. in case readers want to apply for grants from the same organizations

   b. so people know whom to contact for more information

   c. to thank the organizations for their help

Extension

Discuss these questions with a partner or small group, or write a paragraph of response for each.

1. Do you think more money should be spent on developing crops that can respond to the changing climate, or on stopping or reversing global warming?

2. What are some challenges that researchers might face in getting the new strain or rice to the farmers who need it? How could these challenges be overcome?

Reading 2: Education

Pre-Reading Activities

Reading Skills Review

Match the reading skill on the left to its description on the right. If you have forgotten how to use some of the skills, check the explanations again. Then practice all of the skills for the final reading (in two parts).

1. Annotating as You Read (p. 109) ____

2. Dictionary Skills 1: Pronunciation (pp. 51–52) ____

3. Dictionary Skills 2: Recognizing the Right Definition (p. 100) ____

4. Identifying Major and Minor Points (p. 120) ____

5. Identifying Tone: Humor (pp. 86–87) ____

6. Recognizing Support (p. 37) ____

7. Identifying Informed Opinions (p. 74) ____

8. Understanding and Using Charts and Illustrations (pp. 26–27) ____

9. Understanding Transition (pp. 14–15) ____

10. Using Word Parts (p. 61) ____

a. Figure out the part of speech of the unknown word. Pay attention to the context to help you choose the appropriate definition.

b. Look for exaggeration, understatements, sarcasm, and analogies to judge the writer's attitude.

c. Write notes in the margin by each paragraph to summarize the most important ideas.

d. Figure out which ideas in the reading are the most important ones. Then determine which details you need to remember.

e. Check words that link ideas and paragraphs to see the relationship between ideas.

f. Make sure you can pronounce new vocabulary that you need to memorize.

g. Use visual aids in the reading to help you understand difficult concepts or processes, and make sure you can explain them in words.

h. Use the meaning of prefixes, suffixes, and word roots to help you remember the meaning of new vocabulary.

i. Identify the strength of a writer's argument by checking to see if an expert's opinion, facts and statistics, examples, or logical explanations are used.

j. Determine whether the writer is expressing information that can be proven or verified, personal judgments or beliefs, or things that could be either true or argued.

Reviewing Charts

Look at the two charts or bar graphs. Write T if the statement is true or F if the statement is false. Then work with a partner. Write two more true sentences using information from one or both graphs showing data from the USDA. Then share your sentences with another pair.

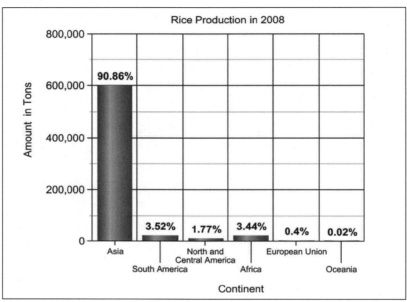

Data from USDA, *PSD Online*, June 2009.

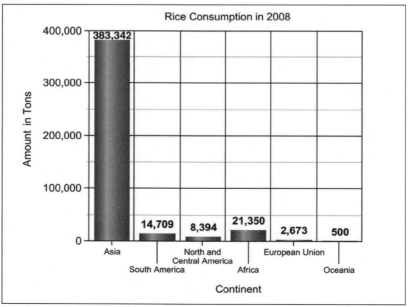

Data from USDA, *PSD Online*, June 2009.

In 2008 . . .

1. _____ Asia produced more rice than any other area.

2. _____ Oceania consumed the least amount of rice.

3. _____ The European Union produced more rice than Africa.

4. _____ Africa consumed more rice than South America, Central America, and North America combined.

5. _____ South America consumed nearly 50,000,000 tons of rice

6. _____ Together, South America, Central America, North America, Africa, the European Union, and Oceania accounted for less than 10 percent of rice production.

Predict

Work with a partner. The next reading (in two parts) is about the mathematics test results of elementary and junior high school students from different countries. What countries do you think scored the highest? Note that you will not find the answer in this first passage; you will read the answer in the second passage later in the unit.

Skim and Scan

The reading passages on pages 132–33 and 135–39 include excerpts from Malcom Gladwell's *Outliers* (2008), which is used as a textbook in some university classes. You don't always need to skim a reading that is this short. This time, just read.

Read

Read the first excerpt from the book. Imagine that you have been asked to read it in a limited time during class. Use all the reading skills you have learned in this book to help you. Use a dictionary only if necessary.

Part 1: The TIMSS Test

Annotations

1 Every four years, an international group of educators administers a comprehensive mathematics and science test to elementary and junior high school students around the world. It's the TIMSS . . . and the point of the TIMSS is to compare the educational achievement of one country with another's.

2 When students sit down to take the TIMSS exam, they also have to fill out a questionnaire. It asks them all kinds of things, such as what their parents' level of education is, and what their views about math are, and what their friends are like. It's not a trivial exercise. It's about 120 questions long. In fact, it is so tedious and demanding that many students leave as many as ten or twenty questions blank.

3 Now, here's the interesting part. As it turns out, the average number of items answered on that questionnaire varies from country to country. It is possible, in fact, to rank all the participating countries according to how many items their students answer on the questionnaire. Now, what do you think happens if you compare the questionnaire rankings with the math rankings on the TIMSS? *They are exactly the same.* In other words, countries whose students are willing to concentrate and sit still long enough and focus on answering every single question in an endless questionnaire are the same countries whose students do the best job of solving math problems.

4 The person who discovered this fact is an education researcher at the University of Pennsylvania named Erling Boe, and he stumbled

across it by accident. "It came out of the blue," he says. Boe hasn't even been able to publish his findings in a scientific journal, because, he says it's just a bit too weird. Remember, he's not saying that the ability to finish the questionnaire and the ability to excel on the math test are related. He's saying that they are *the same*: if you compare the two rankings, they are identical.

5 Think about this another way. Imagine that every year, there was a Math Olympics in some fabulous city in the world. And every country in the world sent its own team of one thousand eight graders. Boe's point is that we could predict precisely the order in which every country would finish in the Math Olympics without asking a single math question. All we would have to do is give them some task measuring how hard they were willing to work. In fact, we wouldn't even have to give them a task. We should be able to predict which countries are best at math simply by looking at which national cultures place the highest emphasis on effort and hard work.

Post-Reading Activities

Understanding the Text

Answer the questions.

1. What point does Gladwell make about the questionnaire administered along with the TIMMS test?

   a. It is important to gather information about the students' backgrounds.

   b. It is long and tedious to complete, so some students choose not to.

   c. It is more difficult than the math questions themselves.

2. What point does Gladwell make about the number of questions students answer on the questionnaire?

   a. The students who answer the most questions do the best on the math questions.

   b. Students from the same country answer different numbers of questions.

   c. The questionnaire tests similar concepts to those on the math test itself.

3. In your own words, what are the main ideas of the passage? Summarize them.

   _____

   _____

   _____

4. Is Gladwell's conclusion that the same countries that value effort and hard work should do best on the math test justified? What kind of support does he use for his argument? Are you convinced by his support? If not, what other kind of support would you like to read?

   _____

   _____

Pre-Reading Activities

Predict

Work with a partner. This unit is about rice. What do you think the author will say about rice that will tie in with his point about the TIMSS test?

Skim

Skim the second excerpt quickly. Check your answer to the Predict question.

Read

Read another excerpt from the book. Use all the reading skills you have learned in this textbook to help you. Decide if you need to annotate the paragraphs in the margins. Use your dictionary if necessary.

Part 2:
Rice Paddies and Math Tests

Annotations

1 Historically, Western agriculture is "mechanically" oriented. In the West, if a farmer wanted to become more efficient or increase his or her yield, he or she introduced more and more sophisticated equipment, which allowed for replacing human labor with mechanical labor: a threshing machine, a hay baler, a combine harvester, a tractor. The farmer cleared another field and increased acreage because now the machinery allowed the farmer to work more land with the same amount of effort. But in Japan or China, farmers didn't have the money to buy equipment—and, in any case, there certainly wasn't any extra land that could easily be converted into new fields. So rice farmers improved their yields by becoming smarter, by being better managers of their own time, and by making better choices. As the anthropologist

Annotations   Francesca Bray puts it, rice agriculture is "skill oriented": if you're willing to weed a bit more diligently, and become more adept at fertilizing,
and spend a bit more time monitoring water levels, and do a better job
keeping the claypan absolutely level, and make use of every square inch
of your rice paddy, you'll harvest a bigger crop. Throughout history, not
surprisingly, the people who grow rice have always worked harder than
almost every other kind of farmer.

2 That last statement might seem a little odd, because most of us
have the sense that everyone in the premodern world worked really
hard. But that simply isn't true. All of us, for example, are descended at
some point from hunter-gatherers, and many hunter-gatherers, by all
accounts, led a pretty leisurely life.

3 [C]onsider the life of a peasant in eighteenth-century Europe. Men
and women in those days probably worked from dawn to noon two
hundred days a year, which works out to about twelve hundred hours
of work annually. During harvest or spring planting, the day might be
longer. In the winter, much less. In *The Discovery of France,* the historian Graham Robb argues that peasant life in a country like France,
even well into the nineteenth century, was essentially brief episodes of
work followed by long periods of idleness.

4 "Ninety-nine percent of all human activity described in this and other
accounts [of French country life]," he writes, took place between late
spring and early autumn." In the Pyrenees and the Alps, entire villages
would essentially hibernate from the time of the first snow in November
until March or April. In more temperate regions of France, where temperatures in the winter rarely fell below freezing the same pattern held. . . .

5 If you were a peasant farmer in Southern China, by contrast, you
didn't sleep through the winter. In the short break marked by the dry season, from November through February, you busied yourself with side
tasks. You made bamboo baskets or hats and sold them in the market.
You repaired the dikes in your rice paddy and rebuilt your mud hut. You
sent one of your sons to work in a nearby village for a relative. You

made tofu and dried bean curd and caught snakes (they were a delicacy) and trapped insects. By the time *lahp cheun* (the "turning of the spring") came, you were back in the fields at dawn. Working in a rice field is ten to twenty times more labor-intensive than working on an

A rice farmer

equivalent-size corn or wheat field. Some estimates put the annual work-load of a wet-rice farmer in Asia at three thousand hours a year.

6 Think, for a moment, about what the life of a rice farmer in the Pearl River Delta must have been like. Three thousand hours a year is a staggering amount of time to spend working, particularly if many of those hours involve being bent over in the hot sun, planting and weeding in a rice paddy.

7 What redeemed the life of a rice farmer, however, was the nature of that work. . . . It was meaningful. First of all, there is a clear relationship in rice farming between effort and reward. The harder you work in a rice field, the more it yields. Second, it's complex work. The rice farmer isn't simply planting in the spring and harvesting in the fall. He or she effectively runs a small business, juggling a family workforce, hedging uncertainty through seed selection, building and managing a sophisticated irrigation system, and coordinating the complicated process of harvesting the first crop while simultaneously preparing the second crop.

8 And most of all, it's autonomous. The peasants of Europe worked essentially as low-paid slaves of an aristocratic landlord, with little control over their own destinies. But China and Japan never developed that kind of oppressive feudal system, because feudalism simply can't work in a rice economy. Growing rice is too complicated and intricate for a system that requires farmers to be coerced and bullied into going out

Annotations

into the fields each morning. By the fourteenth and fifteenth centuries, landlords in central and southern China had an almost completely hands-off relationship with their tenants: they would collect a fixed rent and let farmers go about their business. . . .

A terraced rice paddy

9   The historian David Arkush once compared Russian and Chinese peasant proverbs, and the differences are striking. "If God does not bring it, the earth will not give it" is a typical Russian proverb. That's the kind of fatalism and pessimism typical of a repressive feudal system, where peasants have no reason to believe in the efficacy of their own work. On the other hand, Arkush writes, Chinese proverbs are striking in their belief that "hard work, shrewd planning and self-reliance or cooperation with a small group will in time bring recompense."

10 Here are some of the things that penniless peasants would say to another as they worked three thousand hours a year in the baking heat and humidity of Chinese rice paddies (which, by the way, are filled with leeches):

11 "No food without blood and sweat."

12 "Farmers are busy; farmers are busy; if farmers weren't busy, where would grain to get through the winter come from?"

13 "In winter, the lazy man freezes to death."

14 And, most telling of all: "No one who can rise before dawn three hundred sixty days a year fails to make his family rich." Rise before dawn 360 days a year? For the . . . French peasants sleeping away the

winter, or anyone else living in something other than the world of rice cultivation, that proverb would be unthinkable.

15 This is not, of course, an unfamiliar observation about Asian culture. Go to any Western college campus and you'll find that Asian students have a reputation for being in the library long after everyone else has left. Sometimes people of Asian background get offended when their culture is described this way, because they think that the stereotype is being used as a form of disparagement. But a belief in work ought to be a thing of beauty. . . . Working hard is what successful people do, and the genius of the culture formed in the rice paddies is that hard work gave those in the fields a way to find meaning in the midst of great uncertainty and poverty. That lesson has served Asians well in many endeavors but rarely so perfectly as in the case of mathematics.

* * * * *

16 So, which places are at the top of both lists [the number of questions answered on the TIMSS questionnaire and the math results]? The answer shouldn't surprise you: Singapore, South Korea, China (Taiwan), Hong Kong, and Japan. What those five have in common, of course, is that they are all cultures shaped by the tradition of wet-rice agriculture and meaningful work. They are the kinds of places where, for hundreds of years, penniless peasants, slaving away in the rice paddies three thousand hours a year, said things to one another like "No one who can rise before dawn three hundred sixty days a year fails to make his family rich."

Post-Reading Activities

Main Ideas

Write answers to the questions. Then discuss them with a partner.

1. What are the three reasons Gladwell says that the hard work of growing rice benefited the farmers? Explain in your own words.

2. What do the differences in Russian and Chinese proverbs show?

   _____

   _____

3. Why does Gladwell think that Asian countries score higher on the TIMSS test?

   _____

   _____

Details

Write T if the statement is true or F if the statement is false.

1. Western farmers have depended on machines more than Asian farmers. ____

2. A rice farmer can't do anything to increase the amount of rice he gets from his paddy. ____

3. French peasants in the eighteenth century worked as hard as rice farmers do today. ____

4. European peasants worked about 1,200 hours a year. ____

5. The French peasant farmers did most of their work in the summer. ____

6. Rice farmers in China worked throughout the winter. ____

7. Chinese rice farmers worked about 2,000 hours a year. ____

8. Asian students on Western college campuses are proud that other people see them as hard-working. ____

Vocabulary

Write answers to the questions. Then discuss them with a partner.

1. Were you able to do all of the post-reading exercises without using a dictionary?

2. Skim through the readings again. Which words do you not understand?

3. Do you think they are important words? Which ones do you think you should look up? Which ones are not necessary to know to understand the text?

Reading Skills: Review

Circle the best answer.

1. Read the sentence. What does *by contrast* show?

   If you were a peasant farmer in Southern China, by contrast, you didn't sleep through the winter.

   a. Peasants in China had a harder life than peasants in Europe.
   b. For Chinese peasants, life was harder in the winter.
   c. Chinese peasants in the South had a harder life than those in the North.

2. Which is the most important point about the type of work that Chinese peasants do?
   a. It is meaningful.
   b. It is complex work.
   c. It is autonomous.

3. What do you think the root *soph* means?

   In the West, if a farmer wanted to become more efficient or increase his yield, he introduced more and more sophisticated equipment . . .

   a. simple; easy to use
   b. common; used by many people
   c. wise; wisdom

4. What do you think the root *auto* means?

> *And most of all, [growing rice] is autonomous.*

   a. mechanical; machine-like

   b. self; done by one's own

   c. done without thinking; physical

5. What is the purpose of the underlined part of the sentence?

> *Here are some of the things that penniless peasants would say to another as they worked three thousand hours a year in the baking heat and humidity of Chinese rice paddies (which, by the way, are filled with leeches):*

   a. to emphasize how difficult and unpleasant the work in the rice paddy was

   b. to show that there were some unexpected benefits to working in the rice paddy

   c. to introduce some important information that was left out earlier

6. Label each statement. Write F if the statement is a fact, O if it is an opinion, or IO if it is an informed opinion.

   a. Historically, Western agriculture is "mechanically" oriented. _____

   b. All of us, for example, are descended at some point from hunter-gatherers . . . _____

   c. In the Pyrenees and the Alps, entire villages would essentially hibernate from the time of the first snow in November until March or April. _____

   d. Working in a rice field is ten to twenty times more labor-intensive than working on an equivalent-size corn or wheat field. _____

   e. Growing rice is too complicated and intricate for a system that requires farmers to be coerced and bullied into going out into the fields each morning. _____

   f. Rise before dawn 360 days a year? For the . . . French peasants sleeping away the winter, or anyone else living in something other than the world of rice cultivation, that proverb would be unthinkable. _____

   g. But a belief in work ought to be a thing of beauty. _____

7. Work with a partner. Explain why you would or would not need to learn the pronunciation of the underlined words.

    a. He cleared another field and increased his <u>acreage</u>, because now his machinery allowed him to work more land with the same amount of effort.

    b. Consider the life of a <u>peasant</u> in eighteenth-century Europe.

    c. But China and Japan never developed that kind of oppressive <u>feudal</u> system, because <u>feudalism</u> simply can't work in a rice economy.

    d. That lesson has served Asians well in many <u>endeavors</u> but rarely so perfectly as in the case of mathematics.

8. Work with a partner. Together, check the underlined words below in an English-English dictionary. Write the part of speech above the word and then the correct definition.

    a. So rice farmers improved their <u>yields</u> by becoming smarter by being better managers of their own time, and by making better choices.

    _____

    b. That last statement might seem a little <u>odd</u>, because most of us have the sense that everyone in the premodern world worked really hard.

    _____

    c. In *The Discovery of France*, the historian Graham Robb argues that peasant life in a country like France, even well into the nineteenth century, was essentially <u>brief</u> episodes of work followed by long periods of idleness.

    _____

    d. Ninety-nine percent of all human activity described in this and other <u>accounts</u> [of French country life] . . . took place between late spring and early autumn.

    _____

    e. Three thousand hours a year is a <u>staggering</u> amount of time to spend working.

    _____

Extension

1. Think about what you said initially in answer to this question and decide if your answer is different after reading Part 2 on page 135. Is Gladwell's conclusion, that the same countries that value effort and hard work do best on the math test, justified? What kind of support does he use for his argument? Are you convinced by his support? If not, what other kind of support would you like to read?

2. What advice would you give a student who wished to do better in math, but who did not come from a rice-growing country?

3. Gladwell talks about the high achievement of students from countries that grow rice. In the first reading, however, mention is made of the lack of education and poverty of rice farmers. How do you account for this contradiction?

Answer for Question 4 on page 120:
Top 12 largest consumers of rice:
1. Burma
2. Vietnam
3. Bangladesh
4. Thailand
5. Indonesia
6. Philippines
7. China
8. South Korea
9. India
10. North Korea
11. Japan
12. Taiwan
Data from United States Department of Agriculture. Available from:
www.nationmaster.com/graph/arg_gra_ric_con_percap-grains-of-rice-consumption-per-capita.